Advanced Higher ENGLISH
TEXTUAL ANALYSIS
WITH ADVICE ON CREATIVE WRITING

Ann Bridges and Susan MacDonald

FREE WEB RESOURCES

SCOTTISH EXAMINATION MATERIALS

HODDER GIBSON
AN HACHETTE UK COMPANY

Acknowledgements

Please see the back of the book for a list of all text acknowledgments.

Running head image reproduced on pages 1, 2, 39, 75, 106, 137 and 147 (online) © Christopher Hall - 123RF.com

Although every effort has been made to ensure that website addresses are correct at time of going to press, Hodder Gibson cannot be held responsible for the content of any website mentioned in this book. It is sometimes possible to find a relocated web page by typing in the address of the home page for a website in the URL window of your browser.

Hachette UK's policy is to use papers that are natural, renewable and recyclable products and made from wood grown in sustainable forests. The logging and manufacturing processes are expected to conform to the environmental regulations of the country of origin.

Orders: please contact Bookpoint Ltd, 130 Park Drive, Milton Park, Abingdon, Oxon OX14 4SE. Telephone: (44) 01235 827720. Fax: (44) 01235 400454. Lines are open 9.00–5.00, Monday to Saturday, with a 24-hour message answering service. Visit our website at www.hoddereducation.co.uk. Hodder Gibson can be contacted direct on: Tel: 0141 333 4650; Fax: 0141 404 8188; email: hoddergibson@hodder.co.uk

© Ann Bridges and Susan MacDonald 2016
First published in 2016 by
Hodder Gibson, an imprint of Hodder Education,
An Hachette UK Company
211 St Vincent Street
Glasgow G2 5QY

Impression number	5	4	3	2	1
Year	2020	2019	2018	2017	2016

Cover photo © Christopher Hall - 123RF.com
Typeset in Minion Regular 12/14.5 by Integra Software Services Pvt. Ltd, Pondicherry, India.
Printed in India

A catalogue record for this title is available from the British Library
ISBN: 978 1 4718 8302 6

CONTENTS

PART THREE
Advice, commentaries and student responses are available exclusively on
the Hodder Gibson website at www.hoddereducation.co.uk/updatesandextras.

The contents of this book form part of the response to the changes in the Advanced Higher English Course in the CfE suite of examinations. For the first time, textual analysis of an unseen passage is a compulsory part of the exam, rather than being an option. As a concomitant of this change, the production of a Creative Writing Portfolio is also compulsory. This book, therefore, deals with the analysis of passages in various genres, and preliminary work in preparation for writing in those genres. The process of generating and co-operatively editing short extracts of pupils' work is illustrated alongside the analysis of the particular genres being studied.

The authors would like to thank Madras College English Department, and especially the Advanced Higher candidates who provided all the creative writing examples for Poetry, Prose Fiction and Drama and the student responses to the practice pieces in Part Two.

INTRODUCTION

Textual analysis

Put simply, the kind of textual analysis described in this book is not the complex and philosophical study pursued in universities – although further reading in that area can refine and deepen your understanding of literary theory – but is, in fact, reading for accurate understanding, deeper appreciation and evaluation of the writer's deployment of literary techniques. The following extract from an essay by Zadie Smith puts the task very well:

Note to readers

A novel is a two-way street, in which the labour required on either side is, in the end, equal. Reading, done properly, is every bit as tough as writing – I really believe that. As for those people who align reading with the essentially passive experience of watching television, they only wish to debase reading and readers. The more accurate analogy is that of the amateur musician placing her sheet music on the stand and preparing to play. She must use her own, hard-won, skills to play this piece of music. The greater the skill, the greater the gift she gives the composer and the composer gives her.

… Reading is a skill and an art and readers should take pride in their abilities and have no shame in cultivating them if for no other reason than the fact that writers need you … The ideal reader steps up to the plate of the writer's style so that together writer and reader might hit the ball out of the park.

Creative writing

There are aspects of Zadie Smith's note which can be extended to the skill of creative writing. Especially noteworthy is the comment about the amateur musician. If you have skill in music, or sport, or art, you build on these by practising them. You cannot play a violin sonata if you have not practised for some hours each week – ditto with sports. Writing, too, is a craft. You will have practised this during the course of your English lessons, as you have taken part in music lessons and PE, but none of these is enough by itself. You may have a creative imagination, and have incredibly important ideas and feelings to communicate, but unless you have mastered the craft of writing, you will only be partially successful.

Part One of this book, therefore, tries to address both of these aspects, analysis and creation, together. Most of the short extracts for analysis exemplify one aspect of the writer's technique in each of four genres: poetry, prose fiction, prose non-fiction and drama. A number of these aspects are followed by a short writing task involving the skills required for writing in poetry, fiction, reflectively and in drama. The skills required for writing persuasively or discursively are not dealt with specifically here – they require those skills you have practised throughout your writing career allied with the development of wider research, selective skills and a deeper knowledge and understanding of your topic.

Part Two has longer extracts for practice in responding to a text, allowing you to demonstrate your understanding and your skills in analysis. You will find guidance on understanding and analysis, along with an evaluative student response, for each of the extracts in Part Two on the Hodder Gibson website at www.hoddereducation.co.uk/updatesandextras.

POETRY

Introduction

You will find a wide variety of poems in this section. Not all of them will appeal to you (that is personal taste), but hopefully you will find some that you like. It is important, however, to try all of them because they are used to show a range of useful analytical approaches.

The first section on form or structure is quite extensive, but studying poems in different forms can give you confidence when faced with an unseen poem which has an obvious form or pattern. You can start from a position of some familiarity with how form works. But recognising and being able to name a particular form or specific technique (such as a pattern of rhyme, or use of sound) is not as important as recognising its effect on the meaning of the poem.

If you come across technical terms with which you are not familiar, it is an easy task, in the world of the internet, to find explanations and examples.

As in the other sections of the book, the most important advice is that in order to engage fully with the poem or extract, you write on it. Use the margin or make notes on any and all aspects of the poem to give you something to work with when you draw your thoughts together. Notes and marked up versions of some of the poems are given, but you should really resist using these notes until you have exhausted your own analysis. The notes are there, not as answers but as a way of engaging you in a sort of a conversation with someone else who sees other ideas than perhaps you did in the poems.

One useful approach to textual analysis is to see it as a complement to creative writing. The two skills work well together. You may be a better critic than writer. Or your creative skills may be better than your analytical ones. Being able to do a bit of both is good practice.

> all they want to do
> is tie the poem to a chair with rope
> and torture a confession out of it.
>
> They begin beating it with a hose
> to find out what it really means.–
>
> *Billy Collins,* Introduction to Poetry *(1988)*

Sometimes it seems as if this is a description of how readers analyse a poem in an attempt to understand it. That is not what we are about to do here.

A better comparison for understanding poetry is opening a door – a door into a room of possibilities, of pleasure, of ideas. To open the door, however, you need a key. In this chapter there are notes on some of the 'keys' or poetic techniques that might help open doors to some poems for you, leading to your better understanding.

These poems have been selected to provide examples and stimulation, and one hopes that using these poems to practise analysis will not spoil your enjoyment of them, but rather enhance your appreciation.

Keep that goal of enjoyment in mind as you approach these poems.

Keys

You should be familiar already with some of the techniques or keys for analysing poetry. The following are the most important and useful:

- form or structure
- persona/speaker/point of view
- tone
- word choice/imagery
- rhythm/rhyme/sound.

There is a knack to finding the best key (or keys) for each poem.

Key: form – sonnet

One of the most useful first steps to take in approaching a poem is simply to look at it.

Can you recognise a form? Or can you see a pattern?

Certain forms can be recognised easily and the form itself can lead you to a clearer understanding of the poem and an appreciation of the poet's skill.

First, just look at the poem below and try to see a pattern.

Sonnet 73

That time of year thou mayst in me behold
When yellow leaves, or none, or few, do hang
Upon those boughs which shake against the cold,
Bare ruined choirs*, where late the sweet birds sang.

5   In me thou see'st the twilight of such day
As after sunset faded in the west,
Which by and by black night doth take away,
Death's second self, that seals up all in rest.

In me thou see'st the glowing of such fire,
10   That on the ashes of his youth doth lie,
As the death-bed whereon it must expire
Consumed with that which it was nourished by.

This thou perceiv'st, which makes thy love more strong,
To love that well which thou must leave 'ere long.
William Shakespeare

* 'ruined choirs' could refer to ruined church buildings

Initial thoughts

At first reading this poem may seem difficult. The archaic language ('thou mayst' and 'thou see'st') can be off-putting, to say the least. Overcome that by 'translating' some words into your own language: for example, 'you may see in me that time of year when ...'

But how does the poem *look*?

You cannot help but notice that there is an obvious form or pattern and the rhyming words at the end of the lines establish a pattern within the fourteen lines of the sonnet: three verses of four lines (quatrains) which rhyme abab cdcd efef and then there are two lines at the end (a couplet) which rhyme gg (and they are really puzzling).

When you see breaks in poetry – between verses or stanzas – it is a good idea to look for the differences between the parts. Why does the poet break at these points? (The same question can be asked in fiction or non-fiction passages about the writer's use of paragraphs.)

It is also good to look for similarities or even repetition from one part to the next. What is the continuing idea or the common thought or emotion which runs between verses? Try to make the form work for you to increase your understanding and appreciation of the ideas.

With these ideas in mind, go through these fourteen lines, marking up the poem by writing notes on it as you go along:

1 Note the repetitions from one quatrain to the next.
2 Note, briefly, the subject matter of each verse.
3 Make notes on the word choice in each verse.
4 Make notes on the imagery in each verse.
5 Look for any similarities in the types of words and images used. Also look for any differences.

Compare your notes to the ones below

1 repetition of phrase 'in me' in each quatrain establishes a poetic voice
2 subject of each verse:
   • *first* quatrain is about a time of year – autumn
   • *second* is about a time of day – twilight
   • *third* is puzzling – about a dying fire? An hour or a minute perhaps?
3 words are chosen which have to do with life and death and also colour:
   • *first* quatrain has yellow leaves/bare branches of a tree in autumn and
   • also sound of birds that sang there recently in a 'ruined choir'
   • negative connotations in word 'hang' and 'cold'
   • *second* describes the fading sunset – only suggests colour
   • dark words 'black' and 'night'
   • absence of sounds
   • negative idea in 'Death's second self' and 'rest' – is that sleep?
   • *third* is more difficult, but talks about dying embers of a fire
   • mentions 'ashes of youth' and 'death bed' – both very negative
   • final line is puzzling – 'Consumed with that which it was nourished by'
4 imagery
   • is the poet using a length of time in each verse to represent:
   • stage of life 'in me'? We say an older person is in the autumn of his life
   • or we sometimes talk about being in his twilight years
   • 'autumn' – nearing end of the year
   • 'twilight' – the end of the day
   • 'glowing fire' – the brief moment before it dies

Try to form some ideas about the similarities and differences to help you. For example, periods of time become shorter; colours become less vivid or black; idea of sound disappears; there is more and more mention of sleep; death or death-bed. Try to find meaning in the difficult parts – the puzzles. *Do not ignore the difficult lines.* In this poem the lines at the end of the third quatrain and the final couplet probably require extra thought. You do not need to come up with definite 'answers'. That would be tying the poem to a chair! However, you should have some tentative ideas or suggestions, based on evidence. Learn to be comfortable with speculation and ambiguity. That is the richness of poetry: the openness allows you to have two or three possibilities; further evidence may help you favour one or other of these options.

Summary

This poem has a definite form – the Shakespearean or traditional English sonnet which is instantly recognisable with its fourteen lines, three rhyming quatrains and a final puzzling couplet. This one is written in iambic pentameter and has a 'turning point' (volta) near the end. All these features are characteristic of the traditional sonnet, but poets alter the form to suit their subject and there are as many varieties of sonnets as there are people who write them.

It is important for you to let the form help you in appreciating the ideas. Do not be too concerned about small differences from the traditional pattern. In fact, if there is a difference – a break in the rhyme scheme, a different rhythm, a turning point in the middle rather than at the end – it is probably for a good reason. So look at any adaptation from the traditional form and try to see what effect the change has and why the poet may have chosen to break the pattern.

The quatrains in this sonnet all share the same sort of subject matter – the passage of time, the nearness of death and also the natural imagery of light/darkness and colours and sound, but the tone becomes increasingly darker.

The form and the repetition of the persona 'in me' tie the quatrains together; the subtle differences convey the poet's ideas – the passage of time, transience, brevity of youth? This inevitable change is part of life (and death). A natural cycle. The cruelty of Time is a common Shakespearean theme in his sonnets. The imagery is archetypal – with times of day and year representing phases in life. Sleep is often used as a euphemism for death. (Research the words 'archetype' and 'euphemism' if you are unfamiliar with them).

The final couplet should confirm your thoughts about the poem:

> This thou perceiv'st, which makes thy love more strong,
>
> To love that well which thou must leave 'ere long.

The idea is expressed as a paradox, a bit of a puzzle. That love becomes stronger because nothing lasts forever; or the more you seem to love something or someone, the more intense their loss is and the sooner the loss seems to come about. It is almost as if we burn ourselves out.

You will have your own way of expressing your understanding of the ideas.

Your notes and initial thoughts about the poem give you a good basis for writing about this sonnet.

1 Write a critical analysis of the sonnet in which you explain how the form of the poem has helped in your understanding and appreciation of the ideas. You should also consider aspects such as word choice, imagery and tone.

2 In Shakespeare's day there was a craze among young poets to compete with each other in their composition of sonnets. It was seen as a new and exciting form. It is not difficult to write a sonnet; it does take a lot of thought and redrafting to write a *good* one. Write your own 'Shakespearean sonnet' or some variation of it in which you try to use the form to develop your ideas or reflections on a subject. Usually, the best sonnets impress the reader with the ways in which the verses explore aspects of the same ideas but move towards a climax (or anti-climax) or a conclusion of sorts.

Trying to imitate good writing by applying some of the techniques you have studied can be helpful in recognising and appreciating the effectiveness of such techniques in the work of others.

Sonnet: creative writing

Here is a sample sonnet, written by a student after reading some sonnets. Think about it critically. How effectively has form been used? What changes would you make?

Sunset

The magnificent rays of the setting sun

Broke in on my thoughts of you –

As your memory so often has interrupted my fun

– reminding me of all our days and nights too.

- A 'sonnet' rhyme scheme exists but it is achieved at a price:
- Using unnecessary words e.g., 'too' line 4

5   The orange and vermilion streaks across the sky

Suggest the heat of the warmth between us two

But underneath the leaden streaks across it lie

Reminding me of the quarrels I had with you.

- subverting normal word order, e.g., line 7 (and also lines 9 and 10)

As time passes and darker grows the night

10   So my sadness in my head begins to burgeon

Turning me back into contemplation of my own plight

While all our past overwhelms me like a contagion

Rhythm generally lumpy and difficult to read aloud: lines 1, 3, 4, 11, 12

- clumsy and weak rhyme: 'burgeon' and 'contagion'
- line 13: 'preventing' and 'fighting' used together is not elegant

Preventing me fighting to get you back

And finally at last it all goes black.

Sunset (redrafted)

The dying rays of the setting sun

Break in on my train of thoughts

– As memories of you have often done

Leaving me distracted at your loss.

5   The vermilion streaks across the sky

Suggest the heat that once was ours

But underneath, leaden streaks imply

The painful quarrels of many hours.

As time passes and the night grows dark

10   My sadness burrows deep into my heart

Trying to erase the sorrow – leave no mark.

But all our long past is like a dart

Wounding my will to tempt you back

And finally at last it all goes black.

Variations in the sonnet form

Design

I found a dimpled spider, fat and white,

On a white heal-all, holding up a moth

Like a white piece of rigid satin cloth –

Assorted characters of death and blight

5   Mixed ready to begin the morning right,

Like the ingredients of a witches' broth –

A snow-drop spider, a flower like a froth,

And dead wings carried like a paper kite.

What had that flower to do with being white,

10   The wayside blue and innocent heal-all?

What brought the kindred spider to that height,

Then steered the white moth thither in the night?

What but design of darkness to appall? –

If design govern in a thing so small.

Robert Frost (1936)

Initial thoughts

Now, look at the poem above first and answer these simple questions:

- How many lines are in the poem?
- How are they divided?
- How do they rhyme?

Now read the poem carefully, noting similarities and differences between the first eight lines and the last six lines. Suggest reasons for the division.

Make as many notes about each part of the poem as you can before looking at the marked up version of the poem on page 35.

Check your notes against those you will find there before going on to read the summary below.

Summary

Your notes might include some of the following observations:

1 first part is more visual than the second part
2 second part is more reflective –
3 common feature between the two parts is the ominous note – black magic, witches, and mention of 'design of darkness' in the sestet (the last six lines) is suggestive of the 'witches' broth'
4 word 'design' must be important because it is the title of the poem.

In this sonnet form, the first part of the poem – the octave – seems to set up a situation which allows the persona of the poem – 'I found' – to record his early morning discoveries in nature.

In the second part – the sestet – he reflects and expresses questions/ideas about his discovery.

The octave is descriptive; the sestet is reflective – thinking about the power or design that has engineered the meeting of these three elements of nature. A sort of 'What if?' situation.

In the second part of the poem, the persona of the poem tries to resolve some of the questions raised in the first part.

It is the final line, perhaps, which is most memorable and suggests that he is really thinking about much more than just a spider, a flower and a moth. 'If design govern in a thing so small' leads you to think that he is really beginning to wonder – what design is there for mankind? The choice of words in 'darkness' and 'appall' echo the sinister connotation of 'witches' broth' from the octave and lead to the idea that design is malign or unjust. These might be some of the ideas that you consider.

Redrafting

Poems do not just drop out of the blue. A 'final' version – if there is such a thing – is a result (usually) of many earlier drafts.

Design is a revised version of an earlier poem *In White* by Frost with the same idea and details.

Look at the poems together and list the differences in word choice, sentence structures, imagery.

Think about each difference and which version you prefer and why. Can you suggest why Frost revised his earlier effort? This is a good exercise for helping you to look carefully at language features such as word choice and imagery.

In White

A dented spider like a snow drop white

On a white heal-all, holding up a moth

Like a white piece of lifeless satin cloth –

Saw ever curious eye so strange a slight?

Portent in little, assorted death and blight

Like ingredients of a witches' broth? –

The beady spider, the flower like a froth,

And the moth carried like a paper kite.

What had that flower to do with being white,

The blue prunella every child's delight.

What brought the kindred spider to that height?

(Make we no thesis of the miller's plight.)

What but design of darkness and of night?

Design, design! Do I use the word aright?

Robert Frost (1912)

Design

I found a dimpled spider, fat and white,

On a white heal-all, holding up a moth

Like a white piece of rigid satin cloth –

Assorted characters of death and blight

Mixed ready to begin the morning right,

Like the ingredients of a witches' broth –

A snow-drop spider, a flower like a froth,

And dead wings carried like a paper kite.

What had that flower to do with being white,

The wayside blue and innocent heal-all?

What brought the kindred spider to that height,

Then steered the white moth thither in the night?

What but design of darkness to appall? –

If design govern in a thing so small.

Robert Frost (1936)

1   Write a critical comparison of the two versions of Frost's poem in which you explain the ways in which you find one version more appealing than the other. They both use the same form, but also consider other techniques such as word choice, imagery, structure and title.

2   Redraft a poem (or the sonnet) that you have already written. Make changes to words, imagery, structure and title to experiment and test the effects.

The best way to discover the effectiveness of a form or of any technique is to try to use it in your own writing.

This type of exercise leads to a better understanding of how poetry, in general, works.

Some thoughts about writing your own sonnets

You have seen that it is not just a matter of getting the rhyme right at the end of fourteen rhythmic lines and including a turning point. To be effective, form should not only support, but even help to develop ideas in a poem.

You can also see from the Frost sonnet that further attempts to redraft can improve a poem. After you have the basic ideas and form, you want to return to the creation frequently to consider each word and the structure of each line.

- Does each word or image help to develop your idea?

- Is it consistent with previous words and images?

- Are the ideas in the best order for effect? Perhaps building up to a climax, development or resolution? Or, in some cases, perhaps an anti-climax is appropriate.

- Does the poem sound good – you must say it out loud to test this.

- Does the title fit with the ideas? Is it the best you can do? In a short piece like a sonnet, every word – even the title – has great value.

Key: form – free verse

The traditional English 'Shakespearean' sonnet is one recognisable form. The Frost poem was an 'Italian' or 'Petrarchan' form of the sonnet.

The identification of a particular form of poem by its name is not important in itself; it is the recognition of the ways in which the form supports the content which is the real matter for consideration.

Other forms, such as free verse, can also be helpful in appreciating the ideas of a poem. Even though free verse does not follow the regular rhythm or a more conventional pattern of, for example, a sonnet, it has many and varied possibilities for creating subtle effects. One of its most powerful effects is the placing of a line break at a significant point. For example, in the first two lines of the poem opposite, the break between lines 1 and 2 throws a strong emphasis on 'and death' showing that the acrobat/poet persona is concerned with really important human concerns. Experimentation with free verse in modern times has done much to free poetry from certain formal conventions which might, conceivably, mechanise or regularise it beyond spontaneity.

The Acrobat is a good examle of a poem written in 'free verse'. Mark it up, looking particularly at the effects of the form, but not forgetting other poetic techniques. Then compare your notes with the ones given for this poem on pages 36–37.

Taking a good look at the form as part of your initial reading is always a good approach.

The Acrobat

Constantly risking absurdity
              and death
   whenever he performs
            above the heads
5   of his audience
   the poet like an acrobat
         climbs on rime
           to a high wire of his own making
and balancing on eyebeams
10   above a sea of faces
    paces his way
       to the other side of day
  performing entrechats
        and sleight-of-foot tricks
15 and other high theatrics
        and all without mistaking
     any thing
     for what it may not be

  For he's the super realist
20   who must perforce perceive
    taut truth
      before the taking of each stance or step
in his supposed advance
      toward that still higher perch
25 where Beauty stands and waits
     with gravity
       to start her death-defying leap

  And he
   a little charleychaplin man
30   who may or may not catch
   her fair eternal form
      spreadeagled in the empty air
   of existence
Lawrence Ferlinghetti (1958)

Free verse: creative writing

Following is a student's attempt to use what she has learned from her reading and analysis of *The Acrobat*.

My Kid Brother

One sticky hand pulls my hair, another twists my nose – a round smiling face, snub nose, freckles and a shock of straw-like hair – yes. My kid brother. Coloured feathers, tee shirt and dungarees – a recipe for danger or my affection. I am his god, his mentor, his nemesis and he better not forget it. The heartstrings only stretch so far and when he is older there will be no more excuses for sticky hands, snub noses and even freckles will lose their charm.

This little fragment of descriptive prose has some potential as a poem in free verse, as you can see on the opposite page. The attempt in the first column simply rearranges the form – putting it all into lines – which looks quite good, but is really only lineated prose. The attempt in the second column is much better. The poem has a better arrangement of stages in their relationship. The 'My kid brother' chorus line works – and changes into 'my brother'. And the 'stretch/pull' idea becomes emotional rather than physical. There is also a conclusion which comes as a surprise, and gives the poem a point. It is not now just about her brother; it is 'about' something a bit deeper.

My Kid Brother

One sticky hand pulls my hair

       Another

Twists my nose. A round

       Smiling

Face, snub nose, freckles

       And

A shock of straw-like hair.

       Yes.

My kid brother.

Coloured feathers

       Tee shirt and

       Dungarees

A recipe for danger

       Or

My affection. I am

       His god

His mentor, his nemesis

       And he

Better not forget it

       The heartstrings

Only stretch so far

       And

When he is older

       There

Will be no more

       Excuses.

For sticky hands, snub noses

       And even freckles

will lose their charm.

My Brother

One sticky hand pulls my hair

Another twists my nose,

Next, snub nose and freckles

And a shock of straw-like hair.

Yes.

My kid brother

I am his god, his mentor

At times, his nemesis.

When affection is tested

The heartstrings only stretch

So far,

My kid brother.

When you are older – and bigger –

There will be no more excuses

For sticky hands, or snub noses

Interrupting my sleepy dreams

But for now

My brother

Your freckles still have charm

To enter my heart and pull

Hard –

My brother.

Key: persona

Another key to understanding a poem better can often be identification of the poetic persona or the point of view – the poetic 'voice'.

The persona is the word used to define the 'character' adopted by the poet as the narrator. Sometimes this character is the speaker. At other times the reader is simply using the eyes of this character. The poet is seeing the world through the persona's or 'character's' eyes. In prose fiction we speak about the narrator; in poetry 'persona' is the more appropriate term.

Warning: It is inaccurate to use 'the poet' to identify this persona.

It is even worse to use the actual name of the poet. Remember that the poet is outside of the poem itself; he is detached. He is simply adopting a voice to express thoughts or to relay an experience.

When thinking about persona as a key to a poem, ask yourself these questions:

- Who is speaking?

  This usually involves also identifying the situation or point of view. This might sometimes be the physical/geographical position or situation.

  Or it could, in fact, be an emotional or mental position or outlook.

- Where is he or she or they? Is it important?

- When is this happening? What are the circumstances (if they are important)?

(These are the same questions that you might consider when you are identifying the narrator in prose fiction.)

Warning: It is not always possible (and sometimes not even advisable) to draw definite conclusions about the speaker or persona; you might want to make tentative suggestions. 'The persona may be …'

Look at this short poem by Theodore Roethke (with which you may already be familiar) for a simple example of how the persona works.

Child on Top of a Greenhouse

The wind billowing out the seat of my britches,

My feet crackling splinters of glass and dried putty,

The half-grown chrysanthemums staring up like accusers,

Up through the streaked glass, flashing with sunlight,

A few white clouds all rushing eastward,

A line of elms plunging and tossing like horses,

And everyone, everyone pointing up and shouting!

Theodore Roethke (1948)

Initial thoughts

The word 'my' in the first line tells you that the poem is written from the first-person point of view.

- Who is the 'speaker' or persona?
- Where is the persona?
  (You do not want to say: 'Theodore Roethke is on top of the greenhouse!')
- The title itself, in this case, is almost like a first line in the poem and helps to identify the persona.

You, as a reader, can immediately put yourself in the position of a child, standing on a fragile glass roof ('crackling splinters') in a strong wind and blinding sunlight. A terrifying situation!

Every word is important in this very short poem.

Mark up comments on all the words and images that tell you something about the physical situation of this young child with a short comment for each one. You are looking for all the examples of poetic technique which make the situation vivid and real. Compare your notes with the ones on page 37.

Analysis

- Notice the consistency of words and images – all natural – wind, sun, clouds, horses and flowers.
- Notice the isolation of the child – everyone else, including flowers, pointing up.
- Notice the number of participles ending in 'ing' increasing the sense of activity and excitement.
- And even the final punctuation mark at the end – an exclamation.

This is one brief moment (conveyed in seven lines) of intense excitement and emotion and possibly even guilt!

Summary

The poem is about a physical situation.

A young child has escaped supervision and, in exploring, has reached a position where he is out of control and in danger. From his point of view, he is frightened, not only because of the danger, but also because of the guilt – even the flowers look 'like accusers' and 'everyone, everyone is pointing up and shouting'. Their attention might be for the danger to the child but, from his point of view, it might look as if he is going to be in trouble for his misdeeds. Also, from his point of view, you see details he would notice. In the excitement there is a certain lack of clarity, but there is a lot of movement and light.

Is there also a mental or emotional situation presented here as well as a physical one?

All the words suggest action or danger: the view that the height provides, glass that flashes and trees that plunge and toss 'like wild horses'. The poet very neatly manages to convey the sense of guilt with excitement and thrill that exploration at a young age can stimulate. It is almost as if it is the wrongdoing, the risk itself, that gives the thrill.

All this is achieved by the poet in a very short poem mainly through adopting the point of view of the child, the *persona* of the poem (which is certainly not the poet himself). It might, of course, be a memory from his childhood of such an experience that raised fear and excitement and guilt. He has thought about the best ways of making it vivid and real and *Child on Top of a Greenhouse* is a result.

Think what a different result would have been achieved if he had written in a different point of view, perhaps from the observer looking up at the child. The fear would have been present – fear *for* the child. However, it would not have had the immediacy of the experience with the thrill and sense of wrongdoing as well as terror.

Task

Try writing a short poem in which the persona used, probably first-person, is a key to appreciating the poem. Word choice, imagery, punctuation and even title are still important, but the immediacy of the first-person persona is the technique which helps to make real both a place and a feeling.

First-person persona: creative writing

Child on Top of a Greenhouse has 62 words. You could try in redrafts to cut your poem down to 60–70 words by asking yourself if each word used adds to the value of the poem. Look at the following student example.

On wandering into a church

Coming from outside sunlight –

dim light filtered by coloured glass.

Shapes are hesitant, the eye strains to focus –

first on the gleams, the far away brass, sunbeam lit,

5   then leading back past mysterious shadows

cast by carved tiers of sideways facing benches.

Nearer still a filigree of iron and steps,

leading from the light along a stone pathway

back to me, bathed in the stained light

10   of the high windows behind me.

Calm descends, and then what?

Nothing else happens.

I go.

Commentary

The first-person narrator is being quite accurate about what she sees. The light change, the focus on the far away part leading back to the stained light where she is. Again the 'thought' of the poem leads to the idea that in a church, something should happen. It is calm, might be special – then what – nothing!

To shorten the poem, lines 5 and 6 could come out, but then something would have to be done with 'nearer still'.

In the longer poem *Diving into the Wreck* which follows, the persona which the poet adopts is important in appreciation of the ideas.

Think about the first-person speaker as you read the poem for the first time and the situation in which he (or she) finds himself (or herself). You should be writing on the poem itself, marking up and making notes on all the words and ideas you find thought-provoking or puzzling.

Diving into the Wreck

First having read the book of myths,
and loaded the camera,
and checked the edge of the knife-blade,
I put on
5 the body-armour of black rubber
the absurd flippers
the grave and awkward mask.
I am having to do this
not like Cousteau with his
10 assiduous team
aboard the sun-flooded schooner
but here alone.

There is a ladder.
The ladder is always there
15 hanging innocently
close to the side of the schooner.
We know what it is for,
we who have used it.
Otherwise
20 it is a piece of maritime floss
some sundry equipment.

I go down.
Rung after rung and still
the oxygen immerses me
25 the blue light
the clear atoms
of our human air.
I go down.
My flippers cripple me,
30 I crawl like an insect down the ladder
and there is no one
to tell me when the ocean
will begin.

First the air is blue and then
it is bluer and then green and then   35
black I am blacking out and yet
my mask is powerful
it pumps my blood with power
the sea is another story
the sea is not a question of power   40
I have to learn alone
to turn my body without force
in the deep element.

And now: it is easy to forget
what I came for   45
among so many who have always
lived here
swaying their crenellated fans
between the reefs
and besides   50
you breathe differently down here.

I came to explore the wreck.
The words are purposes.
The words are maps.
I came to see the damage that was done   55
and the treasures that prevail.
I stroke the beam of my lamp
slowly along the flank
of something more permanent
than fish or weed   60

the thing I came for:
the wreck and not the story of the wreck
the thing itself and not the myth
the drowned face always staring
toward the sun   65

the evidence of damage

worn by salt and sway into this
threadbare beauty

the ribs of the disaster

curving their assertion

70 among the tentative haunters.

This is the place.

And I am here, the mermaid whose
dark hair

streams black, the merman in his
armored body.

We circle silently

75 about the wreck

we dive into the hold.

I am she: I am he

whose drowned face sleeps with
open eyes

whose breasts still bear the stress

whose silver, copper, vermeil cargo lies 80

obscurely inside barrels

half-wedged and left to rot

we are the half-destroyed instruments

that once held to a course

the water-eaten log 85

the fouled compass

We are, I am, you are

by cowardice or courage

the one who find our way

back to this scene 90

carrying a knife, a camera

a book of myths

in which

our names do not appear.

Adrienne Rich (1971)

Initial thoughts

Your notes or jottings verse by verse might include some of the following points:

lines 1–12: first word of the poem is 'First' – logical, organised, setting out the problem
- reinforced by actions/verbs of persona – read, loaded, checked and put on
- some puzzles: 'book of myths' – what is it?
- why negative connotations of checking knife-blade – danger? 'body-armour' to describe wet suit, 'mask' also negative – disguise?
- words 'grave' (two meanings) and 'awkward'
- comparison to Cousteau with his team on a sunny schooner to this persona who is alone

lines 13–21: description of ladder – personification – 'hanging' (negative word) 'innocently' sounds suspicious?

lines 22–33: short, simple sentences – 'I go down' – repeated
- immersion in a different world: blue light – clear atoms
- comparison of persona to an insect: crawling, vulnerable, moving slowly

lines 34–43: word 'First' again – starting in a new realm or world – persona trying to think logically
- colours blue, green, black – repeated – seem eerie
- persona has feeling of fainting – although the mask is working with its oxygen
- thinks about force and power – movements are not forceful in this element/the sea
- mentions being alone again

lines 44–51: 'And now' – signals change. What did she come for?
- observations of other things that live here: fish, underwater creatures, 'crenellated fans' and 'reefs'
- 'you breathe differently down here' – uses word 'you' and repeats idea that this is another world

lines 52–60: answers question – 'I came to explore the wreck.'
- short simple sentences: 'words are purposes' and 'words are maps'
- another answer: came to see the damage that was done and what treasures are there
- description of action of moving light of torch along the ship
- personification of ship – 'flank' – and more permanent than fish or weed, living things

lines 61–70: enjambment between verses for first time – one action flows into the next – like swimming around hulk?
- repeats again: came for the wreck – but 'not the story of the wreck'
- repeats 'myth' again: came for the thing itself – not the story
- distressing images of drowned face staring towards sun
- other evidence of time and sea wearing away – 'threadbare beauty'
- personification again in ribs
- question – tentative haunters

lines 71–77: short simple statements – 'This is the place.' 'And I am here'
- questions again: mermaid and merman
- who is 'we'?
- reminded of quiet: 'circle silently', 'dive into the hold'

lines 78–86: again, enjambment – I am she/he – as she looks at 'drowned face' with 'open eyes'.
- description of the wreck of the hold: silver, copper, vermeil – green with algae?
- barrels rotting, instruments decaying, water-eaten log books and an encrusted compass

lines 87–94: now the poet brings together all three pronouns – We, I, you. Who does she mean? Everyone?
- awkward line: 'the one who find our way' – 'one' doesn't seem to fit with 'our'
- then back to the scene at the very beginning – in reverse order – the knife, and camera, and the book of myths
- puzzling last line: our names do not appear in the book of myths?

Analysis

Reading and marking the poem line by line is revealing and helps in appreciating the ideas.

A number of puzzles arise and you do not want to ignore these problems in your analysis; nor do you want to make strong guesses, perhaps, at what the poet intends. You want to speculate, using evidence.

What possible meanings are there?

Which seem the most likely?

Which can be supported by other evidence in the poem?

What sort of interpretation do you get if you read different ideas into the puzzles?

In many poems there is a fair chance that the poet is not trying to give answers, but rather to reflect and to wonder. The most engaging poems are often the ones that raise questions, rather than provide answers. Always think about the evidence. There can be a plurality of interpretations, so the evidence on which you base your comments is important.

So, what are the problems or the puzzles here? There are a few!

Who is the persona?

You cannot really tell if it is a man or a woman. Does it matter, do you think?

Lines 'I am she: I am he' – seems to suggest that it doesn't matter. Also, mermaid/ merman.

But why does 'I' become 'We'? – 'We circle silently ... we dive into the hold' – a shared experience?

'We are, I am, you are ... the one' – does this support the same idea?

Both are the same in the end? In the same situation? Do we all end up in a 'wreck' perhaps?

Persona goes back to the scene at the beginning – the book of myths, the camera and the knife – 'our names do not appear'. Does this mean the living as opposed to the dead? Or a record of some action?

Is the poet exploring the idea of death by using the movement from one element to another strange one – the world of water and the wreck? Or is this the idea of separation?

What is the persona doing?

Literally, preparing for and then diving into a wreck.

But he/she says 'I came for the wreck and not the story of the wreck.' What does he mean?

What is the difference? He/she wants to see the real thing – the faces/the ruins?

Why? What is the motivation for the exploration?

Is the poet using the movement into a different element (water) to reflect upon life and death or separation?

The persona is literally diving. But metaphorically, is the 'dive' a movement or moment of reflection into a 'wreck' – into another world, a ruined world of those who have passed into the 'book of myths' – either through death or other separation of some sort?

There are a number of possibilities here, but these are the types of questions and thoughts which may be running through your mind.

Key: tone

There are still many questions to be answered and more work to be done with the words and images of this poem and, particularly, tone. It may be the tone that will help you further to resolve some of the puzzles. When you are approaching a poem through the use of the persona, it is often very helpful to consider tone.

When we think about 'tone' in day-to-day communications, we think of the 'voice' of the speaker. Angry, solemn, serious, playful? You want to be tuned into the tone that the speaker is using. For example, your teacher might say to you, 'You are the clever one, aren't you?' It is pretty important that you can hear the tone in his voice. Is he serious and therefore praising your efforts? Or is he being sarcastic, suggesting that you are missing the point entirely? In our daily communication, we can *hear* the tone in the voice of the speaker.

However, when we are dealing with the printed word, we have to sense the tone or detect it through careful, detailed reading, using other means to work out the tone. As a reader, you are trying to deduce how the persona would say – or think – the ideas you are dealing with. In other words, what is the state of mind of the speaker? Language features, such as word choice, imagery, sentence structures, even punctuation might help to inform on the state of mind.

Some hints on tone in *Diving into the Wreck*:

- the persona is using a lot of 'dark words' – words like knife, grave, body-armour, hanging, words that suggest conflict

- colours are also dim or even dark – blue and bluer, grim, black

- repetition of words like 'alone', 'rung after rung' and 'I go down' – words suggesting a certain fearfulness or tentativeness in the mind of the persona

- even the vowel sound of these words make them sound ominous

Sentence structures are also helpful. The short, declarative sentences – 'I go down'; 'This is the place'; 'I am here'; 'I am she'; 'I am he'; 'We are'; 'I am'; 'you are' – all suggest that the persona is trying to describe carefully, define and control the situation.

Other sentences reinforce the idea that the persona is trying hard to focus on the job at hand, trying not to let fear creep in: 'it is easy to forget what I came for'; 'I came to explore the wreck'; 'the thing I came for'.

Do these words, images and sentences suggest that the tone is fearful but tightly controlled?

Is the mind set on the purpose but, mentally, the persona is having to try very hard to maintain stability in the face of an awesome task or exploration?

Even the careful ordering of activities – 'first', 'tell me when the ocean will begin', 'first the air', 'then black', and 'now' – suggest that the persona is trying very hard to be in control of the sequence of events. The tone, in other words, is serious, intense – perhaps a little too intense?

These observations about tone revealing the mind of the persona are perhaps as important – or even more important – than answering questions like Who? Where? Why? and When? in this poem. It is like reading between the lines.

There is deliberate ambiguity perhaps.

Summary

It seems that the writer is using the persona of the poem in some of the same ways as Roethke used the child on top of a greenhouse. The diver, like the child, is in an extraordinary situation – out of his comfort zone. And the reader is seeing the world – the wreck – through the eyes of the persona, adopting the reflections of the persona. Both poems are about much more than just the place itself – the top of the greenhouse and the wreck. Both seem to be about the mental state of the persona in a place where he is not entirely comfortable, perhaps in a situation of conflict.

A major difference in understanding the two poems comes with the comparative importance of tone. It is a major key to appreciating the ideas of *Diving into the Wreck*.

In *Diving into the Wreck* there is danger – the knife-blade, the armour and mask. It is lonely. There is fear in entering this eerie, alien environment. The short sentences reinforce this idea. Step by step, the persona is entering tentatively this new world and then immersing himself/herself where even breathing is difficult and requires equipment. The short sentences and the repetition suggest that the persona is trying to control fear and to keep to a purpose: 'this is the place', 'I am here', 'the thing I came for'. The persona is troubled about something and trying to explore thoughts and feelings, perhaps about separation from a loved one or the death of someone – in the same way that a diver has to force himself to enter an alien world to make discoveries – perhaps unwanted ones.

Each reader brings his own thoughts to a reading of a poem, leading to a plurality of interpretation. The important thing is to support those thoughts with evidence. There are as many variations in interpretation as there are readers. In fact, your own interpretation might change from one reading to the next. In one reading it might seem like the persona is facing the death of a loved one. On another reading, it might seem more like a divorce or break-up of a relationship. Identifying the actual situation does not matter as much as recognising and appreciating the feelings of the persona in the situation, trying hard to maintain control and to examine 'the wreck' – whatever the wreck might be.

In *Diving into the Wreck* it is important to understand and appreciate Rich's use of persona and tone. The persona is a key that opens a door to appreciation and it is reinforced by the tone. It is also important to keep reminding yourself that the adoption of a persona is a literary technique and not the poet himself. The poet might be writing from experience, but he/she is detached from the immediate situation of the poem.

It is the persona – not the poet – who is over his head in deep water!

These notes and initial thoughts should give you a good basis for writing about this poem.

Connotations, imagery and structure add to the interpretation of the ideas, but the persona has been a key that may help to structure your response.

Write a critical analysis showing how a focus on the persona, particularly, has helped you to reach an appreciation of the ideas conveyed by Adrienne Rich in *Diving into the Wreck*. You should consider how such techniques as word choice, imagery, sentence structures, and title have also enriched your reading of the poem.

Read the poem that follows to give you more experience in working with the persona as a key to appreciation. This poem is very different from *Diving into the Wreck*. It is a good reminder that poems do not have to be serious to provide the reader with some ideas to reflect upon.

Write a critical analysis of the poem opposite in which you show how 'the voice' in the poem (persona and tone), particularly, has helped you to appreciate the ideas of the poem. You may wish to consider how the tone of the speaker is established by thinking about such language features as rhetorical questions, colloquial language, exaggeration, contrasts, anti-climax, listing, prefacing phrases such as 'of course' and 'frankly' and any other features that you think contribute to tone.

To My Favorite 17-Year-Old High School Girl

Do you realize that if you had started

building the Parthenon on the day you were born

you would be all done in only one more year?

Of course, you couldn't have done it alone,

5   so never mind, you're fine just as you are.

You are loved simply for being yourself.

But did you know that at your age Judy Garland

was pulling down $150,000 a picture,

Joan of Arc was leading the French army to victory,

10   and Blaise Pascal had cleaned up his room?

No wait, I mean he had invented the calculator.

Of course, there will be time for all that later in your life

after you come out of your room

and begin to blossom, or at least pick up all your socks.

15   For some reason, I keep remembering that Lady Jane Grey

was Queen of England when she was only fifteen,

but then she was beheaded, so never mind her as a role model.

A few centuries later, when he was your age,

Franz Schubert was doing the dishes for his family

20   but that did not keep him from composing two symphonies,

four operas, and two complete Masses as a youngster.

But of course that was in Austria at the height

of romantic lyricism, not here in the suburbs of Cleveland.

Frankly, who cares if Annie Oakley was a crack shot at 15

25   or if Maria Callas debuted as Tosca at 17?

We think you are special by just being you,

playing with your food and staring into space.

By the way, I lied about Schubert doing the dishes,

but that doesn't mean he never helped out around the house.

Billy Collins (2011)

Key: imagery

The first key we looked at – form – has the advantage that you consider the poem as a whole.

Another way to approach poems is through line-by-line, or even word-by-word, analysis. It is important, however, not to lose the appreciation of the whole poem when going for this kind of analysis. The little pieces – the words or the lines – must be seen as part of a larger picture. When you examined the previous poems, you looked at evidence of word choice and imagery, as well as form, persona and tone. These are all parts which make up the whole.

For example, in the Shakespearean sonnet (page 3) you noted that the connotation of the words became darker as the poem went on. Also, the imagery of time – the year, the day, the moment – considered shorter and shorter periods of time. In *Child on Top of a Greenhouse* (page 14) you observed – among other things – that a lot of the words were participles (ending in 'ing') which gave a feeling of intense movement and activity. Also, you observed that the flowers looked as if they were staring up at the boy 'like accusers'. In *Diving into the Wreck* (pages 17–18) word choice, imagery and sentence structures all featured significantly in the discussion. The darkening words, the short declarative sentences gave an impression of the mind of the persona.

We have examined form in the sonnet; the structure of free verse; the tone of the persona as keys to appreciation. In the two poems which follow these keys apply, but imagery and connotations of the words become further major keys helpful to our understanding.

In this poem by John Keats, the richness of nature, the fullness of the harvest, the expression of the beauty of the scenes is conveyed largely through the imagery the poet uses. You are familiar with identifying images – similes, metaphors, personification …; in fact, you may have encountered this particular poem before. In *To Autumn* the richness of Keats's imagery is as abundant as the joys of the harvest and the surfeit of sensations.

Think on your first reading about how Keats appeals to every sense and what overall effect that has on your reading.

To Autumn

Season of mists and mellow fruitfulness,
    Close bosom-friend of the maturing sun;
Conspiring with him how to load and bless
    With fruit the vines that round the thatch-eves run;
5   To bend with apples the moss'd cottage-trees,
    And fill all fruit with ripeness to the core;
      To swell the gourd, and plump the hazel shells
With a sweet kernel; to set budding more,
    And still more, later flowers for the bees,
10   Until they think warm days will never cease,
      For Summer has o'er-brimm'd their clammy cells.

→

Who hath not seen thee oft amid thy store?

    Sometimes whoever seeks abroad may find

Thee sitting careless on a granary floor,

15   Thy hair soft-lifted by the winnowing wind;

Or on a half-reap'd furrow sound asleep,

    Drows'd with the fume of poppies, while thy hook

      Spares the next swath and all its twined flowers:

And sometimes like a gleaner thou dost keep

20   Steady thy laden head across a brook;

    Or by a cider-press, with patient look,

      Thou watchest the last oozings hours by hours.

Where are the songs of Spring? Ay, where are they?

    Think not of them, thou hast thy music too,—

25   While barred clouds bloom the soft-dying day,

    And touch the stubble plains with rosy hue;

Then in a wailful choir the small gnats mourn

    Among the river sallows, borne aloft

      Or sinking as the light wind lives or dies;

30   And full-grown lambs loud bleat from hilly bourn;

    Hedge-crickets sing; and now with treble soft

    The red-breast whistles from a garden-croft;

      And gathering swallows twitter in the skies.

John Keats (1819)

Initial thoughts

Think about the effectiveness of the imagery. Mark up the poem by jotting down notes in response to the following four questions – *before* you look at the notes in the analysis.

Look at the images in each stanza.

- Can you see any differences in the type of imagery used in each stanza?
- Which senses are appealed to? What are the effects?
- Can you see any movement or development in the imagery throughout the three stanzas?
- What is the significance of the title?

Then think about the contribution that the poet's use of imagery makes to your appreciation of the poem as whole.

Does the imagery help you to understand the ideas that are being expressed in this poem?

Analysis

Here are some of the observations you may have made about imagery:

- poem is rich with imagery that appeals to senses
- even the title 'To Autumn' indicates the season is being personified and this is like a song to autumn who is imagined as a beautiful woman reaping her harvest

First stanza

- imagery is mostly visual depicting fruitfulness of harvest in the vines, apples, gourds, hazel shells, late flowers
- perhaps also appealing to taste – kernels, apples
- stanza is rich with images of countryside – cottages with vines round the eaves, mossy apple trees bending with fruit, colour of the gourds and flowers and fruit
- even sun is personified as friend to autumn
- other notes: list of verbs – 'to load and bless', 'to bend ... and fill', 'to swell ... and plump' – emphasises the activities of the seasons
- also last lines just keep running on without a break (with two 'ands') as if the activities will never cease
- rhyme – ababcdedcce

Second stanza

- imagery of smell and sight and perhaps taste with softness of wind, smells of ripening grain and hay, odour of poppies, perfume of flowers, ripening apples for cider press
- repetition of oozing as juice from apples is extracted
- even sounds of the words in stanza are soft – 'winnowing wind'
- other 'soft' sounds like 's' – 'sound asleep', 'drows'd', 'spares'
- final lines seem to have a regular beat of words of one syllable – like keeping steady the load across a brook
- last line: sounds seem to draw it out longer – 'the last oozings hours by hours'
- rhyme – ababcdecdde

Third stanza

- auditory imagery – remembers songs of spring – but talks about music of autumn
- wailful choir of gnats mourn, lambs (not full grown in autumn) bleating, hedge crickets singing, final sound of redbreast whistling from garden, swallows twittering
- but also visual images connected to dying day and dying year – 'barred clouds' of sunset, 'rosy hue' and final image of swallows gathering in sky before migrating
- sounds of the gnats imitated in vowel sounds – mourn, among, borne aloft, or
- sound of lambs in 'loud bleat'
- quickness of last lines emphasises the sound of the bird's whistle? Reads very fast in 'whistles from a garden croft; And gathering swallows twitter in the skies'
- rhyme – ababcdecdde

Movement or development through the poem

- first stanza sounds like morning with mists still lingering after nightfall, buds, sun
- second stanza sounds like warmth of a sunny, lazy afternoon
- third stanza is sunset, dying light and ending of year of life of lambs and birds

Summary

The imagery is not random in this ode. There is consistency in the nature imagery and movement in time from stanza to stanza. All senses are included with a movement from a lot of visual detail in the first stanza to emphasis on sound in the third.

It is easy to picture the scenes: the cottages rich with fruit and flowers in the first stanza; the heat of sun and warm wind in the granary and at the harvest, drowsing in the fields with the buzz of bees and birdsong in the second; and the final scene with the setting sun over the stubble field, little swarms of gnats rising and falling in the light wind, bleating of lambs from the hillside, song of the birds and the swarm of swallows gathering for migration.

The title of the poem is an indication of the personification of autumn, a poem praising the season.

Because the poem is so rich with all types of sensual imagery, it is very easy to understand the contribution that imagery makes to appreciating the poem and Keats's skill in its creation.

Task

Write a critical analysis of *To Autumn* in which you explain how the imagery of the poem has enhanced your appreciation of the poem.

Haiku: creative writing

Appreciating the imagery that you encounter in your study of textual analysis should improve your own skill in creating effective images that appeal to the senses. You may wish to try this particular form of haiku.

Haiku is a Japanese form of poetry characterised by three qualities:

* division into two asymmetrical parts in a three-line form of 17 syllables in phrases of 5, 7, 5

* focus on nature or a seasonal subject

* juxtaposition between two very different things, e.g. large/small; natural/human.

The challenge is in the compression and brevity. How vivid can you make your image in the syllable limit? The form is traditional, but nowadays many adaptations can be made. This form gives you a good opportunity to create images with impact and appeal. Short, sharp and shocking! (But don't worry too much if you are plus or minus a syllable.)

Here are a few examples:

Gentle summer rain;	sound
scratch, scratch upon the window	rain/stick
with its little stick.	
Harsh grass, brown and hazed	smell
green smell from arched hall of trees;	grass and trees/hall
shade dapples, flutters.	
Snow melts,	cold
and the village overflows	snow/children
with children.	

Fallen flower I see

Returning to its branch –

Ah! A butterfly.

sight

falling flower/butterfly

Small fish in the sea

quick little splinters of life

enjoying themselves.

sight

fish/splinters

Rate your haiku and those of others on a scale of 1 to 5, with 5 having the most impact.

Key: sound, rhythm and rhyme

Sound is another key to poetry that enhances appreciation.

Consider the number of ways in which poets use sound: sounds of words, lines, even rhyme and rhythm. In *To Autumn*, rhyme, rhythm, alliteration, assonance were part of each stanza imitating the sounds being described in the imagery.

Warning: You cannot consider sound on its own and make your comments seem sensible.

For example, you might write:

• 'The poet uses alliteration in the second stanza in "winnowing wind".'

Even worse:

• 'There is assonance in "full brown lambs loud bleat from hilly bourne".'

So what? Sound has to be used to some purpose. Simply to say that Keats is imitating the sound of the wind sounds feeble. To identify assonance without a nod to what effect is achieved is useless. You have to use these pieces of poetic technique in a context to show how your appreciation and understanding of the whole poem has been enhanced.

Sound, rhythm and rhyme are probably the most technical features of poetic analysis, but it is important not to get 'bogged down' in details of identification of metre or types of rhyme or observation of alliteration, assonance or sprung rhythm ... the list of techniques can be very daunting! What is always important is not the identification of a technique, but your comments on the effect of the poet's use of that technique on your appreciation of the poem. For example, how does the rhythm or rhyme or the sibilant 's' sounds enrich the depiction of the scene or ideas?

Sometimes it is the *breaking of a rhythm* that can be important. Attention can be drawn to the word that does not fit the rhythm or the final word that does not rhyme because that word emphasises a particular idea.

In *To Autumn* good critical comment would note that in the second stanza there are many soft sounds that emphasise the heat and drowsiness of the harvest scene – 'sitting careless', 'hair soft-lifted', 'winnowing wind', 'sound asleep', 'drows'd', 'spares', 'swath'. Also the phrase 'watchest the last oozings' seems to emphasise the time it takes to draw out the juice from the apples – and this is confirmed with the repetition in sound and sense by the phrase 'hours by hours'.

Equally effective are the sounds in the third stanza where Keats is writing about 'songs of Spring' compared to 'music' of autumn. For example, repeated vowel sounds (assonance) in:

Then in a wailful choir the small gnats mourn

These vowel sounds effectively suggest or even mimic the hum of small insects on an autumnal evening.

The final lines of that stanza read very quickly, mentioning and imitating sounds of crickets and birds, as the night falls fast and the season is about to pass from autumn to winter:

> Hedge crickets sing; and now with treble soft
>
> The red-breast whistles from a garden-croft;
>
> And gathering swallows twitter in the skies.

Notice how quickly you can read those lines and how soft the sounds are as if they are dying with the light.

Sometimes using the right term can be useful and economical when you are writing a critical response. It is quicker to say 'assonance' than it is to say 'repetition of vowel sounds' or 'iambic pentameter' rather than trying to describe the rhythm of everyday speech. However, it is by no means essential that you name the technique. It is recognition of the effect that is important.

Read this short poem by Robert Browning and consider how much is conveyed in terms of the story, the description of time and place, the suspense, and the ideas through the use of sound, as well as by other language features. It is a very economical piece of poetry.

Meeting at Night

I

The grey sea and the long black land;

And the yellow half-moon large and low;

And the startled little waves that leap

In fiery ringlets from their sleep,

5 As I gain the cove with pushing prow,

And quench its speed i' the slushy sand.

II

Then a mile of warm sea-scented beach;

Three fields to cross till a farm appears;

A tap at the pane, the quick sharp scratch

10 And blue spurt of a lighted match,

And a voice less loud, thro' its joys and fears,

Than the two hearts beating each to each!

Robert Browning (1849)

Task

Write a critical analysis of the ways in which the poet creates a scene and conveys emotion in this short poem. You will find a number of suggestions on page 38.

Speculative approaches to analysing poetry

One Art

The art of losing isn't hard to master;
so many things seem filled with the intent
to be lost that their loss is no disaster.

To lose something every day. Accept the fluster
5   of lost door keys, the hour badly spent.
The art of losing isn't hard to master.

Then practise losing farther, losing faster:
places, and names, and where it was you meant
to travel. None of these will bring disaster.

10   I lost my mother's watch: And look! My last, or
next-to-last, of three loved houses went.
The art of losing isn't hard to master.

I lost two cities, lovely ones, And, vaster,
some realms I owned, two rivers, a continent
15   I miss them, but it wasn't a disaster.

—Even losing you (the joking voice, a gesture
I love) I shan't have lied. It's evident
the art of losing's not too hard to master
though it may look like (*Write* it!) like disaster.
Elizabeth Bishop (1974)

Understanding and appreciation of a poem are the goals, but there are many approaches to this end, as you have seen.

You may like the idea that there is no one way to analyse a poem. There is no 'right' or 'wrong'.

You may like the idea that there is no single 'answer'. Just effective and well-worked interpretations.

Or, you may find this freedom a bit daunting at first.

It is also worth remembering that it is not always necessary to like the poem you are commenting upon. The word 'appreciation' in critical analysis means 'engagement with' the poem. It is possible to engage very fully with a work which you find ultimately puzzling or even dissatisfying but which, nevertheless, has provoked a strong response in you.

The previous poem, *One Art*, could have a number of differing but valid interpretations. Working with it will give you practice and build confidence in your ability to engage with the ideas of a poem. Consider all the 'keys' you have been given. This is a good opportunity to identify the ones that work for you.

After you have read, marked up and analysed the poem, decide which techniques were critical in opening your mind to the ideas of the poem.

Do not look at the notes and analysis until you are satisfied with your own response.

Task

Write a critical analysis of *One Art* by Elizabeth Bishop, making clear what poetic techniques have helped *you* to understand the ideas of the poem.

Initial thoughts

The person speaking seems the victim of loss – 'so many things'. He/she keeps repeating that 'The art of losing isn't hard to master'. The short stanzas then become almost a list of the things the persona has lost:

- objects like door keys
- time ('the hour badly spent')
- the ability to remember names and places and arrangements for things like travel
- a watch and a house!

The poem moves on to 'big' things which seem almost silly:

- cities
- realms, rivers, a continent.

Then the last stanza is different: 'even losing you'.

Analysis

You should have a lot of questions in your mind at this stage which you should begin to try to answer in a tentative way:

- It is easy to see how you can lose items, but how do you 'lose' a house?
- Or even more surprising – a city or a river?
- Why is there so much repetition? The 'art of losing isn't hard to master' and the denial of 'disaster'.
- Why is the last verse different? Losing a person?
- Why does the title say 'One Art'? Which one? Why?

You may have noticed unusual punctuation in the last stanza – parentheses, dash, exclamation.

Also, the rhyme is unusual in the predominance of two-syllable words (like 'faster' and 'disaster') – feminine rhyme.

You might also like to consider the unusual form because, like the sonnet, you can see that it is unusual. Do you recognise it? Don't panic if you don't. You should still comment on it.

- Try to describe it, along with the rhyme scheme.
- What effect does the form and the rhyme scheme have on your reading of the poem?
- What do your tentative answers to all these questions suggest to you about the persona?

In this task you have been given a direction to approach this poem through poetic techniques. Which ones do you think you would choose? If you had been directed to consider aspects such as form and the poetic voice would that have helped in your approach? Some direction can be useful but you may prefer to select for yourself.

The most important thing is to take a lot of notes; do a lot of 'marking up'.

Your detailed notes might look something like this:

- The items being lost seem to be getting greater throughout the poem.
- First, in terms of size and then in terms of importance. Losing door keys every day is not the same as selling a childhood home, perhaps, and moving away.
- Forgetting someone's name is not as significant as losing that person – perhaps through moving away or even through death.
- Mother's watch would have significance because of sentimental value perhaps.
- Could 'watch' be a pun? Loss of a timepiece or loss of the mother's care – perhaps through death?
- Cities, realms, rivers and a continent could be lost through moving away, emigrating or this might be exaggeration.
- Is it a build-up to the final stanza which is different – suggested by the break in stanzaic form; by the use of four lines, not three; by the dash at its beginning; by the parentheses; and by the words 'Even you'? All of these unite to form a climax to the poem.
- The 'you' addressed seems to be, by far, the most important loss of all. This is further emphasised by the details which follow in the brackets – 'the joking voice, a gesture I love'.

Summary

Form

You may or may not know that this poem is in the unusual form of a villanelle. Now that you have considered sonnets, you should be able to analyse critically the ways in which other forms, including the complex villanelle, can be used to good effect. You may not be familiar with the label 'villanelle', but you should still be able to recognise an unusually complex poetic form and make some suggestions about the effect that this has on meaning.

In a villanelle, the poem is divided into five three-line stanzas (tercets) followed by a final four-line stanza. Nineteen lines in total.

The rhyme scheme is: aba aba aba aba aba abba. This, in itself, might strike you as strange and also a bit restrictive.

Furthermore, there is a lot of repetition:

- line one is repeated exactly in lines 6, 12, and 18; and

- line three is repeated in lines 9, 15 and 19.

Therefore, eight of the nineteen lines are almost like a refrain.

You might be wondering why anyone would ever use such a complex form with so much repetition!

Persona/tone of the speaker

If you look at the lines which are repeated, it might give you some idea about the persona or tone.

Line 1 is repeated: 'The art of losing isn't hard to master.'

Line 3, or at least part of line 3, is also repeated: '[loss] is no disaster'

Is there a suggestion here that the persona is trying to control his/her feelings in this tight form – in spite of the fact that the losses are becoming greater? We repeat ourselves when we are trying to convince ourselves and others that something is true: loss is no *disaster*. Although the regular rhyme of the villanelle and the use of feminine rhyme (rhyming on two syllables) gives this poem a feeling of spontaneity and even flippancy, there is a suggestion here that losing *is* hard to master and that loss *is* a disaster.

Rhyme and rhythm

A climax is reached in the final stanza which is different (four lines), introduced by a dash.

The repeated line – 'The art of losing isn't hard to master' – changes in the last stanza to 'The art of losing's not too hard to master'. '– Even losing you'.

The loss of a person does, in fact, seem to be a disaster, no matter what the persona says. Perhaps he/she is forcing him/herself to write a poem '(*Write* it!)' to try to express or suppress the loss of someone he/she loved. Even the punctuation is odd.

Title

One Art? What is the Art? Writing, perhaps? Bishop puts '*Write* it!' in brackets. You can see that there is evidence to support a number of different meanings or variations of meaning in *One Art*. Even one reader – at different stages of life or in different circumstances – might see different things in the same poem. The compression of poetry also gives it value. Great things can come in small packages.

In this poem, *One Art*, there were a number of approaches or 'keys' that you might have chosen:

- The form is unusual, remarkable and adds much to the mood and meaning of the poem.

- Persona and the tone are both fully developed in a way that lends themselves to discussing the ideas of the entire poem.

- Imagery grows and changes throughout the poem – from small to large, from incidentals that seem to become symbols.

- Sound, rhythm, rhyme, title – even the punctuation.

One Art is a good poem to help you to realise the possibilities of critical analysis: the variety of keys or techniques and the plurality of individual, personal interpretations. To go back to the beginning – doors should open with critical analysis of poetry …

Critical analysis of poetry: a summary

Picking a poem apart line by line can be like unravelling knitting stitch by stitch if all appreciation of the final article is lost.

A secret to successful analysis may be to find the key that will work best for you with a particular poem.

- Is it form?

- Is it persona and tone?

- Is it imagery and word choice?

- Is it the rhyme and rhythm, established, or established and then broken?

Start with the key and then the other comments should follow along to support your written appreciation. This may help to retain the 'wholeness' or the integrity of the poem.

It is also important to remember that you are not trying to find 'an answer'. You are writing an evaluative appreciation which is analytical. You do not have to pin the poem down like a butterfly on a board – or tie it to a chair. That would kill the inspiration and art of the poem.

You can, however, include adverse criticisms as well as praise in your evaluation. You could be discovering aspects of the poem that could work better; or, perhaps, do not work well for you. That type of comment is acceptable as long as it is supported by evidence. You can, of course, also include comments about features which are not entirely clear to you. It is usually better if you try to make suggestions about possible meaning, rather than simply ignoring the puzzling parts.

Two additional poems can be found in Part Two, giving you further opportunity to practise using textual analysis techniques.

Poetry: creative writing

These considerations should affect your own writing of poetry as well.

- Which poetic form best suits your subject and why? How can you best use the chosen form?

- What point of view or persona are you adopting? Are you consistent in its use?

- Is your imagery appropriate? Wide-ranging? Appealing to all the senses if appropriate? Is there consistency in your imagery?

- Does the poem/imagery develop? Move from earlier to later, from near to far, or particular to universal?

- Is there a reason why it does so?

- Have you edited your work, cutting out any unnecessary words?

- Have you read it out loud to see if it sounds right?

Always, there should be a reason why you choose a certain word or take a certain stance or adopt a certain rhyme scheme. Your poem should be better for your knowledge of poetic techniques and how you choose to use them.

Mark up for Design *(from page 8)*

Design — Title – important? A plan?

First-person persona

I found a dimpled spider, fat and white,
On a white heal-all, holding up a moth

Three 'characters': spider/white heal-all/moth
All part of nature – all fragile

White – pure

Like a white piece of rigid satin cloth –
Assorted characters of death and blight
Mixed ready to begin the morning right,

- Positive – early/right
- Ominous – black magic
- Melts-snow/blows away-froth
- Negative – dead/blows away – all transient/passing by

Similes

Like the ingredients of a witches' broth –
A snow-drop spider, a flower like a froth,
And dead wings carried like a paper kite.

What had that flower to do with being white,
The wayside blue and innocent heal-all?

Three rhetorical questions

What brought the kindred spider to that height,
Then steered the white moth thither in the night?
What but design of darkness to appall? –
If design govern in a thing so small.

- Flower usually blue – why white?
- Spider – why so high?
- Moth – why fly to web at night?
- Negative words
- Is there a plan?

Mark up for The Acrobat (from page 11)

Note the look of the poem on the page – the text sways from side to side but with a constant darker line down the centre – perhaps representing the tightrope.

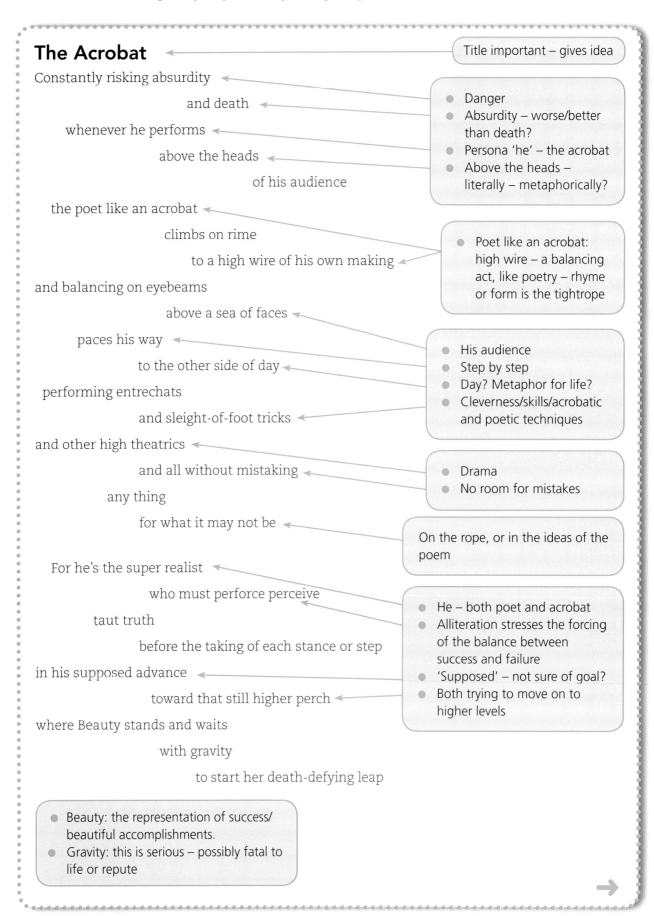

The Acrobat

Title important – gives idea

Constantly risking absurdity

           and death

     whenever he performs

        above the heads

           of his audience

- Danger
- Absurdity – worse/better than death?
- Persona 'he' – the acrobat
- Above the heads – literally – metaphorically?

   the poet like an acrobat

        climbs on rime

          to a high wire of his own making

and balancing on eyebeams

- Poet like an acrobat: high wire – a balancing act, like poetry – rhyme or form is the tightrope

       above a sea of faces

    paces his way

      to the other side of day

   performing entrechats

      and sleight-of-foot tricks

- His audience
- Step by step
- Day? Metaphor for life?
- Cleverness/skills/acrobatic and poetic techniques

and other high theatrics

      and all without mistaking

    any thing

      for what it may not be

- Drama
- No room for mistakes

On the rope, or in the ideas of the poem

   For he's the super realist

       who must perforce perceive

    taut truth

      before the taking of each stance or step

in his supposed advance

      toward that still higher perch

- He – both poet and acrobat
- Alliteration stresses the forcing of the balance between success and failure
- 'Supposed' – not sure of goal?
- Both trying to move on to higher levels

where Beauty stands and waits

     with gravity

      to start her death-defying leap

- Beauty: the representation of success/ beautiful accomplishments.
- Gravity: this is serious – possibly fatal to life or repute

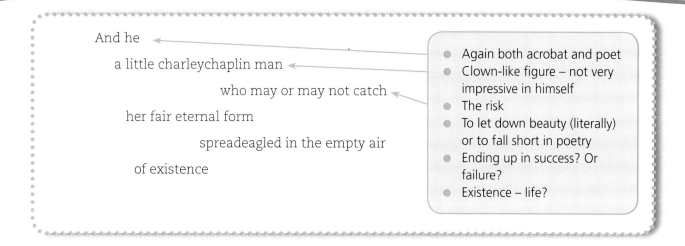

And he
    a little charleychaplin man
        who may or may not catch
    her fair eternal form
        spreadeagled in the empty air
    of existence

- Again both acrobat and poet
- Clown-like figure – not very impressive in himself
- The risk
- To let down beauty (literally) or to fall short in poetry
- Ending up in success? Or failure?
- Existence – life?

The whole poem is an extended metaphor likening acrobat to poet – skill/risk/balance. Beauty is the goal.

The look on the page imitates the tightrope act, making excellent use of a free verse form.

Mark up for Child on Top of a Greenhouse *(from page 14)*

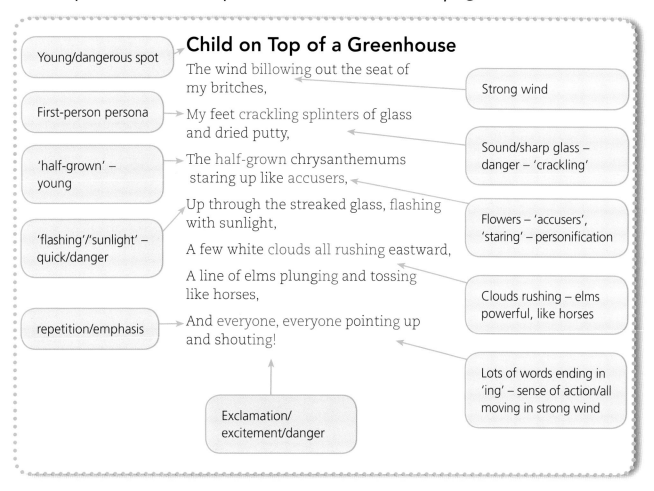

Child on Top of a Greenhouse

Young/dangerous spot

The wind billowing out the seat of
my britches,

Strong wind

First-person persona

My feet crackling splinters of glass
and dried putty,

Sound/sharp glass –
danger – 'crackling'

'half-grown' –
young

The half-grown chrysanthemums
staring up like accusers,

Up through the streaked glass, flashing
with sunlight,

Flowers – 'accusers',
'staring' – personification

'flashing'/'sunlight' –
quick/danger

A few white clouds all rushing eastward,

A line of elms plunging and tossing
like horses,

Clouds rushing – elms
powerful, like horses

repetition/emphasis

And everyone, everyone pointing up
and shouting!

Lots of words ending in
'ing' – sense of action/all
moving in strong wind

Exclamation/
excitement/danger

Mark up for Meeting at Night *(from page 29)*

Meeting at Night

I

- Simple title – naming event
- Sea scene/ approach to land
- Colours subdued
- Personified natural objects – waves
- Persona 'I'
- Use of 'And'

The grey sea and the long black land;

And the yellow half-moon large and low;

And the startled little waves that leap

In fiery ringlets from their sleep,

As I gain the cove with pushing prow,

And quench its speed i' the slushy sand

Sound
- Rhyme scheme: abccba deffed
- 'Fiery' – in moonlight
- Alliteration: 'pushing prow' – pulsing waves?
- Slushy sand – watery sound
- 'Quench' – actual sound of word

II

- Stanza break marks change from sea to land
- Journey by land and meeting
- 'Then' – time
- 'Three fields' – distance
- Repeated use of 'And'
- 'Hearts' – doesn't mention people

Then a mile of warm sea-scented beach;

Three fields to cross till a farm appears;

A tap at the pane, the quick sharp scratch

And blue spurt of a lighted match,

And a voice less loud, thro' its joys and fears,

Than the two hearts beating each to each!

Senses
- 'Sea-scented' – smell
- 'Tap'/'scratch' – 'spurt' sound
- 'Blue'/light – sight
- Alliteration: less loud – quiet sound
- Emotion in exclamation mark

PART ONE

PROSE FICTION

Introduction

The following passages from fiction – complete short stories and extracts from longer works – provide opportunities to study specific techniques of prose fiction. Each passage concentrates on a specific technique but, of course, all passages can be used to demonstrate the use of other aspects. For example, an extract in which you are asked to focus on character may also provide you with good examples of the use of setting, or climax, or any of the other techniques which will be dealt with.

The basic approach which works for all these passages is reading with concentration, 'marking up' what seem to you to be important areas/sentences/phrases – words, even – that help you to understand the content and evaluate the techniques the writer uses.

Through practice and trial and error you will find a method of 'marking up' which suits you. It may be the use of highlighters, or underlining, or writing notes in the margin: what matters is that having a pen (or pencil) in your hand keeps your mind focused on the task and makes your reading active, rather than passive.

After we have looked at the first exercise in this section you will see an example of one method of completing this 'marking-up' task.

Openings

This is the opening of the novel *The Grown-ups* by Victoria Glendinning (1989).

> There's more to love than fucking.
>
> Clara didn't say that aloud, not to Martha.
>
> Leo had been dead a week. The two of them were picking over a pile of newspaper cuttings and Clara was remembering walking on Clapham Common with Leo on a
> 5   windy day, years ago. They both walked self-consciously, arms swinging at their sides, Clara's fingers stiff with longing and indecision. If she put her hand in his, there could be shock, an explosion, an illumination – or just nothing, no connection, embarrassment. She didn't risk it. Leo snapped the lead on to Mungo's collar, and they went back to the house, and to Martha.
>
> 10   Clara turned up the obituary from *The Times*:
>
> *DR LEO ULM*
>
> *Dr Leo Ulm, D Phil, FRSL, who died in the early hours of October 16th his fifty-ninth birthday, was a gifted scholar and a natural communicator who emerged with the new generation of bright young academics in the 1960s and became increasingly prominent in the forefront of intellectual*
> 15   *life in Britain and abroad until the onset of illness earlier this year.* →

> *He was born in Manchester in 1928, the only son of Camelot Ulm, a textile wholesaler …*
>
> Clara skipped the long middle bit about his education, his books, his charm, his career in TV and his university posts, and read the very end:
>
> 20 *In 1954 he married Charlotte Bench-Markham, only daughter of Brigadier F. R. O. Bench-Markham of Belwood in East Sussex. There was one son of the marriage, which was dissolved in 1975. The same year he married Martha Pardo, the illustrator, who survives him.*
>
> 'I never knew Charlotte's name was Bench-Markham,' said Clara.
>
> 25 'So what?' said Martha. 'There was no need for you to know, was there?'
>
> 'One knows hundreds of things one doesn't need to know. Including some things one would rather not know.'

Initial thoughts

This seems to be a fairly straightforward introduction to three characters: Clara, Martha and Leo, who has just died.

A useful way to approach all the extracts in this section is to ask yourself some basic questions to make sure that you have a solid understanding of what the extract is about before you go on to analyse the techniques the writer has used.

The basic questions are:

Who? Where? When? What? followed later by Why? and How?

If we apply this idea to the passage:

Who?

Three characters. Martha is Leo's widow. Clara appears to be a close friend – she is in Martha's house and they are discussing Leo and his obituary.

Where?

The general impression is in England – possibly London (Clapham Common).

When?

The date of publication and the dates given in the obituary suggest that the novel is set in the 1980s. **Note:** always look carefully at the introduction to the extract.

What?

Setting the beginning of the book at the time of Leo's death, and presumably going on to deal with his life, or his relationships with Martha and Clara, among other things.

Why?

The question of what the novel is 'about' – what are the central concerns likely to be – sometimes can't be answered from the information in a short extract. It is difficult to deduce much from this extract, but possibly: marriage/ambition/career/relationships … success or failure?

How?

The writer uses dialogue and description to sketch character and she uses the technique of citing 'outside' sources to give us a lot of information very economically.

The device of the obituary allows us to get, in very few words, the life story of Leo.

Even more skilful is the break in the reading of the obituary: 'Clara skipped the long middle bit about his education, his books, his charm, his career in TV and his university posts, and read the very end.'

This gives an even more economical transfer of information from the writer to the reader – this list really contains more important and interesting facts about Leo than the reference to the actual obituary has done.

Analysis

On second reading, however, there are some points which are a little more enigmatic.

Look again at lines 1–9.

- The opening line is striking. The use of strong language seems a little unconventional in what appears to be a rather conventional setting.
- The flashback to Clapham Common suggests that there might have been a potential relationship between Leo and Clara, which might or might not have progressed to a sexual one.

Was this possible relationship one-sided?

Is there evidence that it wasn't?

- 'both … self-consciously'– suggests there is some awkwardness in the air;
- Leo 'snapped' the lead – suggests that he too had been feeling a tension;
- 'and they went back to the house, <u>and to</u> Martha.'

Always be suspicious of a structure or order of words which is not 'normal' – the writer will have chosen the 'non-standard' form for her own purposes. The standard form would be:

'and they went back to the house and Martha.'

The subtle difference in the use of the comma and the 'to' suggest that going back to Martha is a more conscious (and possibly unwelcome) decision.

It is possible now to look at the first line and see that Clara is suggesting that an unconsummated love affair can be as powerful as a consummated one.

Look again at the last three lines which also seem enigmatic:

'So what?' said Martha. 'There was no need for you to know, was there?'

'One knows hundreds of things one doesn't need to know. Including some things one would rather not know.'

Martha's line suggests that there are parts of her life with Leo which were none of Clara's business – not the friendliest response to a seemingly innocent comment.

Clara's reply suggests that she knows a little too much about some things – possibly Martha and Leo's relationship.

The title *The Grown-ups* is itself enigmatic. Does it mean that everyone behaves in a mature stiff-upper-lip way; or the opposite? **Note:** always look back at the title – often it pinpoints some concern of the text.

Narrative point of view: What Clara thinks or says suggests that the narrative is focusing on her. The narrator is a third-person narrator, and is presumably reliable (we have no reason to think otherwise at the moment). The narrator seems to be giving us Clara's point of view (we don't know what Martha is thinking, for example).

In answer to the question, all the above is relevant. As an opening it is highly effective in that it gives a great deal of background detail in a short passage by means of an external source – in this case the obituary.

Careful reading of the characterisation reveals a possible triangular relationship between the two women and Leo, with some seeds of conflict – 'hooks' to encourage the reader to read on. The first chapter of *Spies*, by Michael Frayn, offers many of the same features as the opening of *The Grown-ups* with the addition of intriguing 'hooks'.

Note: In every case where you make a statement, or give an opinion, evidence from the text should be quoted in support.

Marking up

On first reading, you are on the lookout for anything to help you with the basic who/when/etc. questions, but you are also looking for clues which will help answer a question such us 'How effective is this passage as an opening to the novel?'.

Odd first line/ Shocking?/What does it mean?	There's more to love than fucking.
	Clara didn't say that aloud, not to Martha.

Leo's emotion is involved in some way

Leo had been dead a week. The two of them were picking over a pile of newspaper cuttings and Clara was remembering walking on Clapham Common with Leo on a windy day, years ago. They both walked self-consciously, arms swinging at their sides, Clara's fingers stiff with longing and indecision. If she put her hand in his, there could be shock, an explosion, an illumination – or just nothing, no connection, embarrassment. She didn't risk it. Leo snapped the lead on to Mungo's collar, and they went back to the house, and to Martha.

Tells you about an unspoken (?) desire on Clara's part

Did she ever say or do anything about it?

Suggests some sort of emotion

Clara turned up the obituary from *The Times*:

Odd word order – emphasizing what?

DR LEO ULM

Lots of information here

Dr Leo Ulm, D Phil, FRSL, who died in the early hours of October 16th his fifty-ninth birthday, was a gifted scholar and a natural communicator who emerged with the new generation of bright young academics in the 1960s and became increasingly prominent in the forefront of intellectual life in Britain and abroad until the onset of illness earlier this year.

He was born in Manchester in 1928, the only son of Camelot Ulm, a textile wholesaler …

> These details are very important

Clara skipped the long middle bit about his education, his books, his charm, his career in TV and his university posts, and read the very end:

In 1954 he married Charlotte Bench-Markham, only daughter of Brigadier F. R. O. Bench-Markham of Belwood in East Sussex. There was one son of the marriage, which was dissolved in 1975. The same year he married Martha Pardo, the illustrator, who survives him.

> Gives us information about Martha – second wife, artistic occupation

'I never knew Charlotte's name was Bench-Markham,' said Clara.

'So what?' said Martha. There was no need for you to know, was there?'

> Some sort of annoyance/ coldness. What are these lines about?

'One knows hundreds of things one doesn't need to know. Including some things one would rather not know.'

You are looking for:

- important elements at the beginning and the end of an extract/story
- sections/phrases that you do not understand on first reading – they are likely to be important, so note them for further study
- narrative voice; tone
- structural points – paragraphing, turning points, climax
- elements of characterisation – often words suggesting emotional states
- imagery, symbolism.

These techniques will be explored in later extracts in this section, and will increase your ability to see more, and see more quickly, as you read.

How you make your notes is entirely up to you. Colour has been used in this example, but the use of different types of highlighting or circling, or notes in the margin, or underlining or any combination of these can be helpful.

Openings: creative writing

Having studied this opening, the next task is for you to try writing an opening for yourself.

Then, you should apply the same skills of analysis to your own (or your fellow students') work by editing.

In these first examples, the original and the edited versions are printed beside each other. In all the other examples in the prose fiction section, the editing is done on the same principles, using the same colours, replacements, deletions etc.

Original version

Stepping into the room I understood.

On the dressing table, amidst the many gels, sprays and perfumes was a half-empty bottle of body spray. Open and obviously still in use.

Scratched into the headboard of the bed and barely hidden by an old towel were 4 tiny letters encapsulated by a heart.

'Are you alright?'

I looked at her. The buttons of her shirt were fastened from the wrong side and the sleeves hung low past her tiny wrists. I suddenly remembered the silence that cloaked the air that afternoon when I told her how nice she looked draped under all that material.

Of course, he may be gone, but he was still here.

Edited version

~~Stepping into the room I understood.~~ I stepped into the room. I understood.

On the dressing table, amidst the many gels, sprays and perfumes was a half empty bottle of that body spray. Open and obviously still in use.

~~Scratched into the headboard of the bed and barely hidden by an old towel were 4 tiny letters encapsulated by a heart.~~

'Are you alright?'

I looked at her. The buttons of her shirt were fastened from the wrong side and the sleeves hung low past her ~~tiny~~ wrists. I suddenly remembered the silence that cloaked the air that afternoon when I told her how nice she looked draped under all that material.

Of course, he may be gone, but he was still here.

> Starting with a participle – 'stepping' is weaker than 'I stepped'. Breaking the first sentence into two allows the eye to stop on the 'bottle of body spray' (which is obviously important; using 'that' helps. The headboard bit makes things too obvious. The man's shirt clue is more subtle – whose shirt? Last sentence has a nice ambiguity. 'Tiny' is vastly and lazily overused. The green words or phrases are not quite right and should be replaced.
>
> **What happens next?** It looks like the 'eternal triangle' – two men/one woman.

Original version

The ground seemed to tremble as feet thudded upon it in haphazard motion.

The trees laced together as if deliberately making themselves more difficult to navigate through, thorns and branches sticking out at all angles. One breath at the wrong time could spell catastrophe.

Her breath pounded through her body as she tried to plan her next move, the famous questions: flee or fight? The pain in her leg seemed to radiate through every thought she attempted to have, making it impossibly more difficult to come to a decision. Glancing around hurriedly she noticed the sky progressively getting darker and more desolate, sealing her decision to flee. A sudden scurrying noise startled her into movement, and at once she was on her way again, hoping soon to escape her fate.

→

Edited version

The ground seemed to ~~tremble~~ resound as her feet thudded upon it in haphazard motion.

The ~~trees~~ branches laced together as if deliberately making themselves more difficult to navigate. ~~through, thorns and branches sticking out at all angles.~~ One too deep breath at the wrong time could spell catastrophe.

~~Her breath pounded through~~ Suppressed gasps wracked her body as she tried to plan her next move, the famous questions: flee or fight? The pain in her leg ~~seemed to~~ radiated through her every thought ~~she attempted to have~~, making it impossibly ~~more~~ difficult to come to a decision. ~~Glancing around hurriedly she noticed~~ But the sky ~~progressively~~ was getting darker and more desolate, sealing her ~~decision~~ choice to flee. A sudden scurrying noise startled her into movement, and at once she was on her way again, limping, stumbling, hoping soon to escape her fate.

> The whole sequence suggests sound is the problem, therefore 'resound' rather than 'tremble'; whose feet?; trees don't lace – branches can; thorns etc. too much; 'too deep' needed for idea of loud sound; idea of 'suppressed gasps' has more sound content than (physiologically impossible?) breath pounding; 'seemed' nearly always weakens meaning; 'her' neater than the alternative; 'seemed' 'noticed' 'decided' are usually weak or redundant; 'progressively … getting darker' is tautological; 'decision' is used in previous sentence therefore 'choice'; addition of 'limping, stumbling' adds to idea of injury and desperation – and three participles in sequence gives a sense of climax.
>
> **What happens next?** Has to be escape, or immediate capture with dire consequences …

Characterisation

A

The following is an extract from the beginning of a short story by Stan Barstow – *The Actor* (1961). Just after the events described here Albert is asked to take the part of a policeman in the local dramatic society's production of a play.

> He was a big man, without surplus flesh, and with an impassivity of face that hid extreme shyness, and which, allied with his striking build, made him look more than anything else, as he walked home-wards in the early evening in fawn mackintosh and trilby hat, like a plain-clothes policeman going quietly and efficiently about his business,
> 5   with trouble for someone at the end of it.
>
> All his adult life people had been saying to him, 'You should have been a policeman, Mr. Royston,' or, more familiarly, 'You've missed your way, Albert. You're cut out for a copper, lad.' But he would smile in his quiet patient way, as though no one had ever said it before, and almost always give exactly the same reply: 'Nay, I'm all right. I like my bed at nights.'
>
> →

10   In reality he was a shop assistant and could be found, in a white smock, on five and a half days of the week behind the counter of the Moorend branch grocery store of Cressley Industrial Cooperative Society, where he was assistant manager. He had been assistant manager for five years and seemed fated to occupy that position for many years to come before the promotion earmarked for him would become a fact, for the
15   manager was a man of settled disposition also, and comparatively young and fit.

But Albert did not apparently worry. He did not apparently worry about anything; but this again was the deception of his appearance. Quiet he might be, and stolid and settled in his ways; but no one but he had known the agony of shyness that was his wedding day; and no one but he had known the pure terror of the premature birth of his only
20   child, when the dead baby he longed for with so much secret yearning had almost cost the life of the one person without whom his own life would hardly have seemed possible – Alice, his wife.

So it was with the measure of his misleading appearance and his ability to hide his feelings that no one ever guessed the truth, that no one was ever led from the belief that
25   he was a taciturn man of unshakeable placidity. 'You want to take a leaf out of Albert's book,' they would say. 'Take a lesson from him. Never worries, Albert doesn't.'

Thus Albert, at the age of thirty-seven, on the eve of his small adventure.

Task

Think about the means by which the character of Albert is presented to the reader. While reading the extract, and before you go on to look at the advice, mark those words/phrases/paragraphs that help with your understanding of Albert.

Initial thoughts

In this introduction to the short story you are given a character Albert, who is obviously going to be key – and almost certainly 'The Actor' of the title. The answers to the usual questions are not too difficult to find in this case. You will find a summary of them after the paragraph by paragraph approach shown here.

In this case, paragraphing is an important help to your understanding of the steps the writer is taking to introduce the character of Albert gradually:

- physical description
- what the character says
- what he does, what he thinks
- what others say about him
- his setting in time and place
- the role of the narrator (in this case, the narrator appears to be a reliable third-person narrator who lets us into Albert's thought processes).

Analysis

Lines 1–5

Which two important aspects of character are set up in these lines?

'Big', 'impassivity', 'striking build' – suggesting a solid, good citizen with a powerful presence.

But, 'hid extreme shyness' is equally important.

Normally, in your own creative writing pieces, you are taught that physical description of a character has to have some relevance to the story/characterisation as a whole. Here a whole paragraph is devoted to his appearance, but each part of the description is relevant because the resemblance to a policeman is going to be relevant to the story of 'The Actor'.

Lines 6–9

This paragraph emphasises the policeman idea, but the most important aspect is another 'emotional' clue – 'as though no one had ever said it before'. This reinforces one of the ideas from the first paragraph – that he manages to hide his frustration at the repetitive nature of the comments.

Lines 10–15

Two important words are given to you at the beginning – 'In reality'. This signals a contrast from the 'fantasy policeman'.

All the suggestions in these lines are that he has a very 'ordinary' (possibly boring or monotonous) life.

How does the structure and word choice push you towards this idea?

'[T]he Moorend branch grocery store of Cressley Industrial Cooperative Society' – why all the detail? Try reading it out loud. There is a suggestion of the monotony or the sameness or the unadventurous nature of his job. None of these names is in any way exotic or romantic – just ordinary industrial northern English town names.

Repetition of 'assistant manager' – emphasises the unchanging nature of his employment. 'settled disposition also' not only applies to the manger but to Albert as well.

Lines 16–22

This paragraph comes as a bit of a surprise – the vocabulary changes from stolid, safe, 'settled' descriptive words to much more emotionally charged ones: 'agony', 'pure terror', 'yearning'.

But the change is signalled by the repetition of the word 'apparently'.

The word order of the long sentence beginning 'Quiet he might be … Alice, his wife' is particularly carefully chosen.

When normal English word order is disrupted, the unexpected order usually packs a punch. The normal word order at the beginning of the sentence would be 'He might be quiet and stolid and settled …'. What is gained by the change?

It puts emphasis on his 'quietness' which is hiding something (see first paragraph) and the placing at the end of the sentence – at its climax – 'Alice, his wife' instead of 'his wife Alice' gives her more weight in Albert's story.

Lines 23–26

This paragraph brings together the two sides of Albert which we met in the first paragraph – 'his misleading appearance' and 'his ability to hide his feelings' – so that the reader is prepared for these aspects to reappear in some important way in the rest of the story.

Line 27

A beautifully economic paragraph which lets us know that we are 'at the end of the beginning' in structural terms, and that now the story will launch onto the central incident – 'his small adventure'.

In **structural** terms, the opening of each paragraph gives us a clear series of steps leading us towards the story: 'He was …'; 'All his adult life …'; 'In reality …'; 'But …'; 'So …'; 'Thus …'.

Note: In every case where a statement has been made there is evidence quoted from the text in support.

Summary

Who? Albert and Alice (obviously a strong relationship) and, presumably, some members of the local dramatic society.

Where? An industrial midland/northern town.

When? Written in 1961, and not sci-fi or futuristic, therefore before then. But no apparent trauma or poverty, therefore probably after the Second World War. So probably the 1950s. The more you know of history, social history, politics, period drama etc., the more likely you are to be able to place events in their social and economic background.

What? We don't know yet, except that it will involve Albert, an amateur dramatic society, the part of a policeman, and probably some sort of disappointment for Albert which he will then 'hide' from everyone.

Why? The central concern is possibly exploring the 'agony of shyness' and people's lack of understanding and sympathy with the condition.

How? Characterisation; narrative hooks; social setting; paragraph structure; sentence structure; word choice.

B

The following is the beginning of Chapter 1 of *Dombey and Son* (1848) by Charles Dickens – slightly adapted.

Dombey sat in the corner of the darkened room in the great arm-chair by the bedside, and Son lay tucked up warm in a little basket bedstead, carefully disposed on a low settee immediately in front of the fire and close to it, as if his constitution were analogous to that of a muffin, and it was essential to toast him brown while he
5   was very new.

Dombey was about eight-and-forty years of age. Son about eight-and-forty minutes. Dombey was rather bald, rather red, and though a handsome well-made man, too stern and pompous in appearance, to be prepossessing. Son was very bald, and very red, and though (of course) an undeniably fine infant, somewhat crushed and spotty in his
10   general effect, as yet.

Dombey, exulting in the long-looked-for event, jingled and jingled the heavy gold watch-chain that depended from below his trim blue coat, whereof the buttons sparkled phosphorescently in the feeble rays of the distant fire. Son, with his little fists curled up and clenched, seemed, in his feeble way, to be squaring at existence for having come
15   upon him so unexpectedly.

'The House will once again, Mrs Dombey,' said Mr Dombey, 'be not only in name but in fact Dombey and Son;' and he added, in a tone of luxurious satisfaction, with his eyes half-closed as if he were reading the name in a device of flowers, and inhaling their fragrance at the same time; 'Dom-bey and Son!'

20   The words had such a softening influence, that he appended a term of endearment to Mrs Dombey's name (though not without some hesitation, as being a man but little used to that form of address): and said, 'Mrs Dombey, my—my dear.'

A transient flush of faint surprise overspread the sick lady's face as she raised her eyes towards him.

25   'He will be christened Paul, my—Mrs Dombey—of course.'

She feebly echoed, 'Of course,' or rather expressed it by the motion of her lips, and closed her eyes again.

Those three words conveyed the one idea of Mr Dombey's life. The earth was made for Dombey and Son to trade in, and the sun and moon were made to give them light. Rivers
30   and seas were formed to float their ships; rainbows gave them promise of fair weather; winds blew for or against their enterprises; stars and planets circled in their orbits, to preserve inviolate a system of which they were the centre.

He had risen, as his father had before him, in the course of life and death, from Son to Dombey, and for nearly twenty years had been the sole representative of the Firm. Of
35   those years he had been married, ten—married, as some said, to a lady with no heart to give him; whose happiness was in the past, and who was content to bind her broken spirit to the dutiful and meek endurance of the present. Such idle talk was little likely to reach the ears of Mr Dombey, whom it nearly concerned; and probably no one in the world would have received it with such utter incredulity as he, if it had reached him.
40   Dombey and Son had often dealt in hides, but never in hearts. They left that fancy ware to boys and girls, and boarding-schools and books. Mr Dombey would have reasoned: That a matrimonial alliance with himself *must*, in the nature of things, be gratifying and

45 honourable to any woman of common sense. That the hope of giving birth to a new partner in such a House, could not fail to awaken a glorious and stirring ambition in the breast of the least ambitious of her sex. That Mrs Dombey had entered on that social contract of matrimony – almost necessarily part of a genteel and wealthy station, even without reference to the perpetuation of family Firms – with her eyes fully open to these advantages. That Mrs Dombey had had daily practical knowledge of his position in society. That Mrs Dombey had always sat at the head of his table, and done the honours

50 of his house in a remarkably lady-like and becoming manner. That Mrs Dombey must have been happy. That she couldn't help it.

Or, at all events, with one drawback. Yes. That he would have allowed. With only one; but that one certainly involving much. They had been married ten years, and until this present day on which Mr Dombey sat jingling and jingling his heavy gold watch-chain in

55 the great arm-chair by the side of the bed, had had no issue.

—To speak of; none worth mentioning. There had been a girl some six years before, and the child, who had stolen into the chamber unobserved, was now crouching timidly, in a corner whence she could see her mother's face. But what was a girl to Dombey and Son! In the capital of the House's name and dignity, such a child was merely a piece of base

60 coin that couldn't be invested—a bad Boy—nothing more.

Mr Dombey's cup of satisfaction was so full at this moment, however, that he felt he could afford a drop or two of its contents, even to sprinkle on the dust in the by-path of his little daughter.

So he said, 'Florence, you may go and look at your pretty brother, if you like, I daresay.

65 Don't touch him!'

The child glanced keenly at the blue coat and stiff white cravat, which, with a pair of creaking boots and a very loud ticking watch, embodied her idea of a father; but her eyes returned to her mother's face immediately, and she neither moved nor answered.

Next moment, the lady had opened her eyes and seen the child; and the child had run

70 towards her; and, standing on tiptoe, the better to hide her face in her embrace, had clung about her with a desperate affection very much at variance with her years.

'Oh Lord bless me!' said Mr Dombey, rising testily. 'A very ill-advised and feverish proceeding this, I am sure. I had better ask Doctor Peps if he'll have the goodness to step upstairs again perhaps. I'll go down. I'll go down. I needn't beg you,' he added,

75 pausing for a moment at the settee before the fire, 'to take particular care of this young gentleman, Mrs ——'

'Blockitt, Sir?' suggested the nurse, a simpering piece of faded gentility, who did not presume to state her name as a fact, but merely offered it as a mild suggestion.

'Of this young gentleman, Mrs Blockitt.'

80 'No, Sir, indeed. I remember when Miss Florence was born—'

'Ay, ay, ay,' said Mr Dombey, bending over the basket bedstead, and slightly bending his brows at the same time. 'Miss Florence was all very well, but this is another matter. This young gentleman has to accomplish a destiny. A destiny, little fellow!' As he thus apostrophised the infant he raised one of his hands to his lips, and kissed it;

85 then, seeming to fear that the action involved some compromise of his dignity, went, awkwardly enough, away.

Think about how Mr Dombey's character is presented in this extract from the beginning of the novel. While reading the extract again, and before you go on to look at the comments below, mark in each paragraph – except perhaps the first – at least one sentence, phrase or word which gives an insight into Mr Dombey's character.

Initial thoughts

The general impression is of a man totally self-satisfied and self-absorbed in his own selfish world, in which a son is necessary to the continuance of the central concept of his life – the firm of Dombey and Son. (The fact that the title of the book is 'Dombey and Son' lends emphasis to this obsession.)

The questions as to who, what period, what is happening are all easily answered here – there is no puzzle. The passage seems to suggest that the central concerns are likely to be more sombre than the birth of a child would suggest.

Analysis

There is an obvious tone and narrative point of view.

It is always important to consider these two aspects in every text you read.

Tone: has elements of humour – 'as if his constitution were analogous to that of a muffin, and it was essential to toast him brown while he was very new'.

The fact that he is referred to as Son as opposed to merely son suggests that he represents something much bigger than himself in his father's eyes.

Narrative point of view is ironically critical of Dombey: 'too stern and pompous in appearance to be prepossessing'.

Remember to produce evidence for each statement you make.

Possible evidence for his self-satisfaction:

'Exulting' with the parallel suggestion that everything in his world is shining – 'gold watch-chain', 'buttons sparkled phosphorescently', 'luxurious satisfaction, with his eyes half-closed as if … inhaling their fragrance'.

Possible evidence for his pomposity:

His wife is surprised that he adds 'my – my dear' – and the hesitation shows that he is totally unaccustomed to addressing her as anything except 'Mrs Dombey'. He can't quite keep it up, however, reverting to 'Mrs Dombey' in the next paragraph.

Possible evidence for his self-aggrandisement:

His elevated idea of his importance is shown, for example, in lines 28–32, where the language of the Old Testament story of the Creation is echoed in his description of the importance of the firm 'Dombey and Son'.

Possible evidence for his lack of empathy:

His relationship with Mrs Dombey is dealt with in lines 33–51. These lines show his complete ignorance of his wife's feelings – and lack of any kind of empathy – 'Dombey and Son had often dealt in hides, but never in hearts.'

His fixation on the Son is shown even more clearly in the next two paragraphs: 'They had been married ten years … had had no issue. —To speak of; none worth mentioning. There had been a girl some six years before …' and 'such a child was … —a bad Boy— nothing more'.

His fixation on the world of finance and commerce could be evidenced by the extended metaphor used here to describe Florence:

'In the capital of the House's name and dignity, such a child was merely a piece of base coin that couldn't be invested—a bad Boy—nothing more.'

His relationship with his daughter is obviously distant:

'The blue coat and stiff white cravat … creaking … very loud ticking watch, embodied her idea of a father' – the choice of words all being rather frightening, certainly not soft or affectionate.

His complete favouring of the boy over the girl is shown in the incident where Florence runs to her mother and emotionally embraces her 'desperately' – causing Mr Dombey to think only of this as being bad for his wife because it might be upsetting to the baby.

And 'Miss Florence is all very well, but this is another matter. This young gentleman has to accomplish a destiny.'

His action at the end where he actually kisses the hand of the baby shows how unable he is to demonstrate affection of any kind – as he thinks it a bit weak and that it might demean him in the eyes of the world – 'some compromise of his dignity, went, awkwardly enough, away'.

Summary

You could sum up by noting that overall, as the passage goes on, there is less humour and the view of Mr Dombey becomes ever more critical – especially shown in his treatment of Florence.

You could also think about how effective this is as an opening to the novel – as dealt with on pages 39–43.

Characterisation: creative writing

Having studied the presentation of character, the next task is for you to make your own attempt to introduce a character.

Then, you should apply the same skills of analysis to your own (or your fellow students') work by editing.

In these examples, the original and the edited version are printed as one piece. The editing is done on the same principles, using the same colours, replacements, deletions etc. as demonstrated on pages 44–45.

Rosie

The bus jittered to a halt and Rosie stepped on. As she did so, she found herself temporarily blinded by the harsh lights of the bus – ~~which proved to be~~ a strong contrast to the murky ~~black~~ world that surrounded the ~~rusty~~ vehicle. She walked up the aisle with small ~~yet sure~~ steps, ignoring the ~~piercing~~ stares of the eyes that were
5   glued upon her ~~person~~. She was a vision of dreary colour – a vision of antique brasses and artichokes and dark mosses – as if she had gone to all the bother of bringing the darkness onto the bus with her.

When Rosie had finally chosen a seat ~~to sit~~, she flopped ~~her frail body~~ down ~~and~~, inhaled, exhaled. The ~~stale~~ air surrounding her was filled with a thick, sticky smell of
10   stagnant nicotine, which ~~continued to creep~~/crept around the bus ~~until~~/nauseating every passenger ~~felt themselves wince~~. It was ~~worse so~~/worst for the young man who was sitting directly behind her, who had to ~~in fact~~ suppress ~~vocalising~~ his discomfort/with a shudder when ~~poor old~~ Rosie stretched her arms ~~back~~ onto the ~~edge~~/back of her seat. Her fingernails were all stained yellow, except her ~~two~~
15   forefinger~~s~~ which ~~were~~/was a more burnt orange colour. The skin on her hands was thick and cracked, like clay.

'Excuse me' the young man said, in a such a soft voice it was drowned out by the bus' engine. He tried again, ~~and~~ but still without success, ~~decided to tap~~ tapped her bony shoulder.

20   She slowly twisted ~~her spine~~ around to meet his eye. Her skin was sunken and flaccid, ~~it draped over her cheekbones and collected in a billowy bundle at the bottom of her face.~~ but her eyes were sharp, although marked with a feverish restlessness ~~although slightly stained yellow, banana yellow. She had a glossy stare~~, which ~~caused~~ gave her expression ~~to be~~ a mix of ~~complete~~ annoyance and
25   desperation.

'What?!' she demanded.

Commentary

Many redundant adjectives and over-the-top descriptive phrases have been removed.

Verbs such as 'which proved to', 'continued to creep', 'decided to tap', 'caused (her expression) to be', have been replaced by going straight to the action itself: 'crept', 'tapped', 'gave' etc.

Some words have been replaced by better equivalents – 'nauseating' for 'wince'; 'shudder' for 'vocalising'.

The last paragraph has been rewritten to point up the 'desperation' of the woman, to pick up on the rather odd description of her earlier when she '(brought) the darkness onto the bus with her'. These two ideas suggest that the character we have been introduced to is more intriguing/dangerous/interesting than merely the rather disgusting description of an unattractive old woman.

To Catch a Prince

The discussion on the other side of the door was getting louder. So loud in fact, that one might go so far as to call it an argument. Mrs Howard was shouting at Mr
5   Howard, and Mr Howard was shouting at Mrs Howard, and each was making a very good case for Catherine's failure being the fault of the other. Finally, there was the sound of a sharp smack, an angry shriek and the noise of a door slamming. Catherine breathed a sigh of relief that the argument had at last resolved itself. After waiting a short while, she crept into the lounge to read for herself the offending
10   article. It began with the usual 'Dear Mr and Mrs Howard, we are sorry to have to inform you that Catherine has been suspended from school for three days … ' blah, blah, blah. There was the usual accusations – daydreaming, distracting others, shouting out, talking in class, giggling at the teachers and so on, such minor offences really, she thought, that it's a wonder they bothered writing them out at all. And then
15   there came the truly outrageous accusations: 'Catherine has been partaking in inappropriate conduct with another student … ' Now in her defence Catherine would argue, and she often did, that that word, 'inappropriate', is what is called 'subjective'. 'Subjective', she knew, meant that different people might have different opinions – which might depend on their 'perspective'– and one opinion is not necessarily more
20   right than another opinion. So when someone calls something 'inappropriate' and another does not, she thought, we must all just agree to disagree and leave it at that. It really was terribly unfortunate that Catherine's head teacher was not the diplomat that she was. The letter continued: 'Catherine has also been caught smoking in the girls toilets'. Perhaps true … but just once, only once, and not nearly so much as went on in the teacher's lounge. The letter finished with a request to meet her parents for 'a discussion concerning Catherine's future at the school'. With two enraged fists she
25   scrunched up the letter and threw it on the ground in disgust. It wasn't her fault that she was no good at school. She supposed the problem was that she was just too stupid to learn. Her father said so, her grandmother said so and now even she was saying so. Luckily, Catherine didn't need to be clever. She didn't have the need for anything as trivial as an education. She had long honey coloured hair that reached
30   down almost to her waist and big brown eyes with long eyelashes which she could bat really very effectively. She knew that this was enough – for it certainly had been enough for her mother – to catch a prince. Now she need only find him.

Commentary

This is quite a clever introduction to Catherine's character. It is not just the picture of a rather rebellious and 'stupid' student. The opening description of the 'argument' seems to end in domestic violence – probably her mother being hit by her father – which she does not seem to think is particularly significant or shocking (suggesting that this is normal?).

The last two sentences recall her mother's situation, but she sees herself following her mother's footsteps – using her beauty to 'catch a prince'. The fact that she doesn't see the pitfalls as exemplified by her parents' marriage suggests that she is in for a repeat performance of her mother's life.

The section in the middle where she is commenting on the headmistress' letter has a tone which reveals Catherine as quite knowing and subtle; she is by no means 'stupid' in her justification of her own behaviour.

→

The phrases and sentences in green could probably be improved. For example, 'With two enraged fists she scrunched up the letter and threw it on the ground in disgust.' One feels that Catherine's emotions here do not tie up with her rather 'cool' attitude in the previous section – she might be more likely to use it to make a paper aeroplane. On the other hand, there is some stylish writing – for example, the use of a three-part cadence in 'Her father said so ...'

The structure of this piece needs to be clarified by paragraphing. There appears to be none.

The first paragraph should probably end at 'had at last resolved itself' and the last paragraph should probably start at 'Luckily, Catherine ...'

Or perhaps even the last sentence could be a one-line paragraph for dramatic effect.

This structure would help to point up to the reader the connections between the references to 'mother'.

Structure

A: short story

The following is a complete short story, *The Breadwinner*, written by Leslie Halward (1936).

> The parents of the boy of fourteen were waiting for him to come home with his first week's wages.
>
> The mother had laid the table and was cutting some slices of bread and butter for tea. She was a little woman with a pinched face and a spare body, dressed in a blue blouse and skirt, the front of the skirt covered with a starched white apron. She looked tired and frequently sighed heavily.
>
> The father, sprawling inelegantly in an old armchair by the fireside, legs outstretched, was little too. He had watery blue eyes and a heavy brown moustache, which he sucked occasionally.
>
> These people were plainly poor, for the room, though clean, was meanly furnished, and the thick pieces of bread and butter the only food.
>
> As she prepared the meal, the woman from time to time looked contemptuously at her husband. He ignored her, raising his eyebrows, humming, or tapping his teeth now and then with his finger-nails, making a pretence of being bored.
>
> 'You'll keep your hands off the money,' said the woman, obviously repeating something she had said several times before. 'I know what'll happen to it if you get hold of it. He'll give it to me. It'll pay the rent and buy us a bit of food, and not go into the till at the nearest public-house.'
>
> 'You shut your mouth,' said the man, quietly.

20   'I'll not shut my mouth!' cried the woman, in a quick burst of anger. 'Why should I shut my mouth? You've been boss here long enough. I put up with it when you were bringing money into the house, but I'll not put up with it now. You're nobody here. Understand? *Nobody. I'm* boss and he'll hand the money to me!'

'We'll see about that,' said the man, leisurely poking the fire.

25   Nothing more was said for about five minutes.

Then the boy came in. He did not look older than ten or eleven years. He looked absurd in long trousers. The whites of his eyes against his black face gave him a startled expression.

The father got to his feet.

30   'Where's the money?' he demanded.

The boy looked from one to the other. He was afraid of his father. He licked his pale lips.

'Come on now,' said the man. 'Where's the money?'

'Don't give it to him,' said the woman. 'Don't give it to him, Billy. Give it to me.'

The father advanced on the boy, his teeth showing in a snarl under his big moustache.

35   'Where's that money?' he almost whispered.

The boy looked him straight in the eyes.

'I lost it,' he said.

'You – *what*?' cried his father.

'I lost it,' the boy repeated.

40   The man began to shout and wave his hands about.

'Lost it! *Lost* it! What are you talking about? How could you lose it?'

'It was in a packet,' said the boy, 'a little envelope. I lost it.'

'Where did you lose it?'

'I don't know. I must have dropped it in the street.'

45   'Did you go back and look for it?'

The boy nodded. 'I couldn't find it,' he said.

The man made a noise in his throat, half grunt, half moan – the sort of noise that an animal would make.

'So you lost it, did you?' he said. He stepped back a couple of paces and took off his belt –
50   a wide, thick belt with a heavy brass buckle. 'Come here,' he said.

The boy, biting his lower lip so as to keep back the tears, advanced and the man raised his arm. The woman, motionless until that moment, leapt forward and seized it. Her husband, finding strength in his blind rage, pushed her aside easily. He brought the belt down on the boy's back. He beat him unmercifully about the body and legs. The boy sank
55   to the floor, but did not cry out.

When the man had spent himself, he put on the belt and pulled the boy to his feet.

'Now you'll get off to bed,' he said.

'The lad wants some food,' said the woman.

→

'He'll go to bed. Go and wash yourself.'

60 Without a word the boy went into the scullery and washed his hands and face. When he had done this he went straight upstairs.

The man sat down at the table, ate some bread and butter and drank two cups of tea. The woman ate nothing. She sat opposite him, never taking her eyes from his face, looking with hatred at him. Just as before, he took no notice of her, ignored her, behaved

65 as if she were not there at all.

When he had finished the meal he went out.

Immediately he had shut the door the woman jumped to her feet and ran upstairs to the boy's room.

He was sobbing bitterly, his face buried in the pillow. She sat on the edge of the bed

70 and put her arms about him, pressed him close to her breast, ran her fingers through his disordered hair, whispered endearments, consoling him. He let her do this, finding comfort in her caresses, relief in his own tears.

After a while his weeping ceased. He raised his head and smiled at her, his wet eyes bright. Then he put his hand under the pillow and withdrew a small dirty envelope.

75 'Here's the money,' he whispered.

She took the envelope and opened it and pulled out a long strip of paper with some figures on it – a ten shilling note and a sixpence.

Task

Think about how the structure of this short story helps your understanding of character, plot and central concerns. Before going on to look at the advice which follows, look at each paragraph in lines 1–25, and mark a fact important to characterisation/plot.

Initial thoughts

This is a relatively straightforward short story with a very common structure. You have probably been reading and analysing this kind of story for years. But this story has the virtue of being very short, allowing the structure to be pinpointed accurately.

Generally speaking, in this kind of classically shaped short story you are looking for:

a) introduction, possibly to character/setting/plot
   followed by:

b) a central incident/event/happening which will usually reach some sort of climactic action/conflict/ emotion

c) an ending or a resolution.

Analysis

The task here is to mark the 'end' of the beginning, the 'beginning' of the end, and the point at which you think the climax of the story has been reached.

Not everyone will come to the same conclusion. There are several different possibilities, which can be justified. The important aspect is not so much the points chosen, as the justification you give for choosing them.

The first mark could be placed after line 2 or line 11 or line 25.

Possible justifications:

- Line 2: This first sentence introduces the whole idea of the plot of the story. The Breadwinner of the title is a boy of fourteen whose arrival with the money is the central incident.
- Line 11: The first four paragraphs introduce, respectively, the plot, the mother, the father, and their poverty-stricken circumstances.
- Line 25: The first four paragraphs perform the functions suggested above; and the seeds of the disagreement between husband and wife about the money lead up to the moment when the boy arrives.

The point marking the beginning of the end could be at line 60 or line 69 or line 75.

Possible justifications:

- Line 60: The main incident in the story is finished.
- Line 69: The father has 'left the stage' leaving the mother free to tend to the boy.
- Line 75: The boy reveals his subterfuge, overturning the father's power.

Now, the climax:

Most people would choose the paragraph from lines 45–55 (or possibly 56) because the action which has been threatening, the culmination of the man's anger, has reached its violent conclusion.

(It would be possible to suggest line 66, on the grounds that the tension might be held up until then, as the man could be contemplating more violence – or something unpredictable might happen – and until he leaves the house there is no release or safety.)

Summary

The simplicity of this story allows you very quickly to run through the normal questions:

Who? Mother, father, son. Only the son is given a name. Why?

Where? An industrial town, somewhere. The boy has obviously been doing a dirty manual job.

When? At some time before 1936. What are the clues?

What? There is no need to guess this – in a complete short story you have all the information.

Why? Possibly the central concerns/thematic ideas in this case – the effects of poverty on relationships/exploitation/small victories over oppression …

How? The narrative voice – third-person omniscient – seems to be reliable. There is no sense of any tone which would suggest that it is anything other than a straightforward account.

But there is a bias. Look at the description of the mother (lines 3–6) and the description of the father (lines 7–9). There are aspects of word choice which are meant to prejudice you in favour of the mother before the story even gets under way: 'little', 'spare', 'blue blouse and skirt', 'starched white apron' – these all give the impression of someone who, even in adversity (and she is tired) is intent on maintaining a respectable standard – 'starched' is particularly important. The father, on the other hand, is given 'sprawling inelegantly', 'watery … eyes', 'heavy' and 'sucked'.

Contrast is created between these two characters in these two paragraphs. Again this is a structural point. As we have noticed before, paragraphing is essential to an understanding of how structure works.

Identifying the climax allows the reader to see the height of the conflict between father and son, and identifying the ending allows you to see the relationship between mother and son – and its small triumph.

The title of the story is *The Breadwinner* – the irony is that it is not the father but the fourteen-year-old son who is putting food on the table, and the contrast between the title and the description of the boy in lines 26–28 is intended to draw the reader's attention to the conflict between the boy and the man.

B: chapter

The following chapter is from *Maurice,* a novel by E.M. Forster which was started in 1914 but not published until after Forster's death in 1971. The subject matter which relates to homosexual love was thought by Forster to be unpublishable because homosexuality was illegal in England until 1968.

In Chapter 28, Maurice has come home after university, and has had to change and reconcile himself to a life with his family and a career in the city.

His change, then, cannot be described as a conversion. There was nothing edifying about it. When he came home and examined the pistol he would never use, he was seized with disgust; when he greeted his mother no unfathomable love for her welled up. He lived on, miserable and misunderstood, as before, and increasingly lonely. One cannot write
5   those words too often: Maurice's loneliness: it increased.

But change there had been. He set himself to acquire new habits, and in particular those minor arts of life that he had neglected when with Clive. Punctuality, courtesy, patriotism, chivalry even – here were a few. He practised a severe self-discipline. It was necessary not only to acquire the art, but to know when to apply it, and gently to modify
10   his behaviour. At first he could do little. He had taken up a line to which his family and the world were accustomed, and any deviation worried them. This came out very strongly in a conversation with Ada.

Ada had become engaged to his old chum Chapman, and his hideous rivalry with her could end. Even after his grandfather's death he had feared she might marry Clive, and
15   gone hot with jealousy. Clive would marry someone. But the thought of him with Ada remained maddening, and he could scarcely have behaved properly unless it had been removed.

The match was excellent, and having approved of it publicly, he took her aside and said, 'Ada, I behaved so badly to you, dear, after Clive's visit. I want to say so now and ask you
20   to forgive me. It's given a lot of pain since. I'm very sorry.'

She looked surprised and not quite pleased; he saw that she still disliked him. She muttered, 'That's all over – I love Arthur now.'

'I wish I had not gone mad that evening, but I happened to be very much worried about something. Clive never said what I let you think he said either. He never blamed you.'

25   'I don't care whether he did. It doesn't signify.'

Her brother's apologies were so rare that she seized the opportunity to trample on him. 'When did you last see him?' – Kitty had suggested they had quarrelled.

'Not for some time.'

'Those weekends and Wednesdays seem to have quite stopped.'

30   'I wish you happiness. Old Chappie's a good fellow. For two people who are in love to marry strikes me as very jolly.'

'It's very kind of you to wish me happiness, Maurice, I'm sure. I hope I shall have it whether I am wished it or not.' (This was described to Chapman afterwards as a 'repartee'.) 'I'm sure I wish you the same sort of thing you've been wishing me all
35   along equally.' Her face reddened. She had suffered a good deal, and was by no means indifferent to Clive, whose withdrawal had hurt her.

Similar difficulties arose with Kitty. She also was on his conscience, but was displeased when he made amends. He offered to pay her fees at the Domestic Institute whereon her soul had been so long set, and though she accepted, it was ungraciously, and with the
40   remark, 'I expect I'm too old now to properly learn anything.' She and Ada incited each other to thwart him in little things. Mrs Hall was shocked at first and rebuked them, but finding her son too indifferent to protect himself, she grew indifferent too. She was fond of him, but would not fight for him. And so it happened that he was considered less in the house, and during the winter rather lost the position he had won at Cambridge. It
45   began to be 'Oh, Maurice won't mind – he can walk – sleep on the camp bed – smoke without a fire.' He raised no objection – this was the sort of thing he now lived for – but he noted the subtle change and how it coincided with the coming of loneliness.

The world was likewise puzzled. He joined the Territorials – hitherto he had held off on the ground that the country can only be saved by conscription. He supported the
50   social work even of the Church. He gave up Saturday golf in order to play football with the youths of the College Settlement* in South London, and his Wednesday evenings in order to teach arithmetic and boxing to them. The railway carriage felt a little suspicious. Hall had turned serious, what! He cut down his expenses that he might subscribe more largely to charities – to preventive charities: he would not give a halfpenny to rescue
55   work. What with all this and with his stockbroking he managed to keep on the go.

Yet he was doing a fine thing – proving on how little the soul can exist. Fed neither by Heaven nor by Earth he was going forward, a lamp that would have blown out, were materialism true. He hadn't a God, he hadn't a lover – the two usual incentives to virtue. But on he struggled with his back to ease, because dignity demanded it. There was no
60   one to watch him, nor did he watch himself, but struggles like his are the supreme achievements of humanity, and surpass any legends about Heaven.

No reward awaited him. This work, like much that had gone before, was to fall ruining. But he did not fall with it, and the muscles it had developed remained for another use.

*the College Settlement was a charitable institution supported by the university – a sort of youth club combining sport and education.

Task

Think about how the structure of this chapter helps your understanding of Maurice's character and his relationships with those around him. Mark up the text, identifying as you go how each paragraph deals in some way with either Maurice's feelings/intentions, or his relationships with those with whom he comes into contact. Mark also where you feel the climax of the chapter to be.

Initial thoughts

Who?

Maurice, his mother, sisters Ada and Kitty – Clive and Chapman are mentioned: both as suitors of Ada.

Where and When?

London, contemporaneous with the date of writing.

What?

Maurice's efforts to change his life are recounted. This appears to be the result of a problem to do with Clive.

Why?

The need to understand the central concerns about the exploration of loneliness or some sort of sacrifice of the soul.

How?

The structure plays a major part in your understanding of the relationships within and outside the family. The dialogue in paragraph 4 (lines 18–36) is also helpful.

Analysis

Paragraph structure in this chapter aids our understanding of the steps Maurice takes in his 'change'. Its importance is emphasised by the first two words of the extract: 'His change'. 'His change, then, cannot be described as a conversion' and the opening paragraph goes on to deal with his relationship with his mother. There is the suggestion that he had thought of suicide – 'the pistol' – and then rejected it. But the decision did not make him any less miserable. The last sentence in the paragraph: 'One cannot write those words too often: Maurice's loneliness: it increased.' is using all the power of sentence manipulation to make the reader understand just how lonely Maurice was. Normal word order is replaced by a strong sentence, with its two colons, separating three important statements. The writer is making sure that you have appreciated its depths.

Paragraph 2 also starts with reference to change:

'But change there had been.' This is followed by the idea that he worked hard to become different – 'to modify his behaviour'– as if it were an artificial exercise.

His relationship with Clive has obviously caused his relationship with Ada to fail 'he had feared she might marry Clive, and gone hot with jealousy.'

Paragraph 4 (lines 18–36) shows Maurice's attempt to reconcile himself with Ada (as part of his 'change'). The reception of his apology is not what he might have hoped.

The dialogue in this paragraph also helps to fill in some of the background. He has obviously behaved badly. Ada is not so ready to be reconciled and niggles him about his relationship with Clive by asking awkward questions: 'When did you last see him?' Maurice tries to sidestep the question – 'Not for some time', but when Ada doesn't let it go and makes a comment about 'Those weekends and Wednesdays seem to have quite stopped' he changes the subject completely. This avoidance, along with the mention in paragraph 7 of what he now does on Wednesdays and Saturdays, suggests that he always used to be with Clive at those times.

Paragraph 5 deals with Maurice's attempt by his changed attitude to reconcile himself with Kitty, his other sister, with little success: 'it was ungraciously' accepted. The remainder of the paragraph shows a sort of common front of indifference being shown to him by all three women, Ada, Kitty and his mother. There is a sense in which he almost welcomes their indifference as a punishment for his previous life. This paragraph ends again by commenting on his 'loneliness'.

Paragraph 6 deals with how 'the world' – that is, the people he knows in London, his acquaintances and fellow rail commuters ('The railway carriage') are puzzled by the change in him. All his previous views (about conscription) and pursuits (like golf) have changed to be replaced by charitable works. They felt he had turned 'serious' on them – and perhaps resented the guilt they might have felt at his moral superiority.

Paragraph 7 refutes that idea with 'Yet': he had no sense of moral superiority – the reverse, in fact. 'Yet' also points up the contrast suggested in paragraphs 1 and 2 – that although he was doing good works, and working hard at it, he was not recompensed by any outward or inner rewards. 'But on he struggled with his back to ease, because dignity demanded it.' He was still lonely, 'He hadn't a God, he hadn't a lover' but – and this is probably the climax of the chapter – nothing is working.

'No reward' at the beginning of the last paragraph finishes the chapter on a seemingly negative note – with just a slight ray of hope – that the fortitude he was building up in this artificial way might be of use.

Summary

Each paragraph in this short chapter allows us to clarify what Maurice is trying to do, and how in each of his relationships there is a complete failure of understanding.

Understanding structure is a means to an end – to the understanding of: effectiveness of character portrayal; effectiveness of an opening; effectiveness in opening up a central concern; a meaningful contrast; or an important conflict or climax.

Look back to remind yourself how the paragraph structure helped with characterisation in *The Actor* (pages 45–48).

There are many other structural techniques used by writers of novels and short stories. Two commonly used are:

C: framing

A framing device is where a narrator starts and finishes a short story or novel with her recollection of events, while the story itself could be either her narrative of a time past, or could be someone else's narrative which she is relating. In the case of the framing device, one always has to take into account the reliability of the narrator. An example of this is illustrated in the section on narrative voice (pages 72–73) – *A Tradition of Eighteen Hundred and Four*.

A framing device can also can give your reflective writing a structure which encourages you to put your experience/ideas in a way which requires you to be truly reflective.

D: circular

Some short stories have a kind of circular device where the end of the story recalls the beginning.

This short story by Virginia Woolf, *Ancestors*, demonstrates this circularity.

Mrs Vallance, as Jack Renshaw made that silly, rather conceited remark of his about not liking to watch cricket matches, felt that she must draw his attention somehow, must make him understand, yes, and all the other young people whom she saw, what her father would have said; how different her father and mother, yes and she too were from all this; and how compared to really dignified simple men and women like her father, like her dear mother, all *this* seemed to her so trivial.

Summary of the middle of the story

Mrs Vallance is irritated by the attitudes of the young man Jack Renshaw who says he doesn't like to watch cricket matches and who passes admiring comments on a younger woman's dress. She soothes her irritation with a series of reminiscences about her parents, whose cultivation she sees as superior to her current surroundings. She resuscitates nostalgic images of reverential figures in after-dinner conversations on summer nights conducted under big trees in starlight.

She feels that her parents have instilled in her a sense of beauty, and that they understood her in a way that her present company does not.

If they [her parents] had lived, Mrs Vallance felt that none of this — and she looked at Jack Renshaw and the girl whose clothes he admired — could have had any existence, and she would have been oh perfectly happy, perfectly good, instead of which here she was forced to listen to a young man saying — and she laughed almost scornfully and yet tears were in her eyes — that he could not bear to watch cricket matches!

Commentary

The repetition of Renshaw, and the cricket and the triviality, all part of the first paragraph, are echoed in the final paragraph, where the feelings of Mrs Vallance are more intense, and personally even tragic.

This **circularity** can be transferred to your own writing, in fiction, but it is also a useful technique for crafting a **reflective essay**.

Free indirect speech

The 'voice' of the narrator here is rather more complicated than it looks. It appears to be third-person narrative focused through the character of Mrs Vallance, but there are aspects of first-person narrative – such as 'how different her father and mother, yes and she too were from all this' and 'she would have been oh perfectly happy' – in the speech forms. This style is known as **free indirect speech**.

Setting

The following extract is taken from the beginning of chapter two of *The Handmaid's Tale* by Margaret Atwood (1985).

A chair, a table, a lamp. Above, on the white ceiling, a relief ornament in the shape of a wreath, and in the centre a blank space, plastered over, like the place in the face where the eye has been taken out. There must have been a chandelier, once. They've removed anything you could tie a rope to.

5 A window, two white curtains. Under the window, a window seat with a little cushion. When the window is partly open – it only opens partly – the air can come in and make the curtains move. I can sit in the chair, or in the window seat, hands folded, and watch this. Sunlight comes in through the window too, and falls on the floor, which is made of wood, in narrow strips, highly polished. I can smell the polish. There's a rug on the floor,

10 oval, of braided rags. This is the kind of touch they like: folk art, archaic, made by women, in their spare time, from things that have no further use. A return to traditional values. Waste not want not. I am not being wasted. Why do I want?

On the wall above the chair, a picture, framed but with no glass: a print of flowers, blue irises, watercolour. Flowers are still allowed. Does each of us have the same print, the

15 same chair, the same white curtains, I wonder? Government issue?

Think of it as being in the army, said Aunt Lydia.

A bed. Single, mattress medium-hard, covered with a flocked white spread. Nothing takes place in the bed but sleep; or no sleep. I try not to think too much. Like other things now, thought must be rationed. There's a lot that doesn't bear thinking about. Thinking can

20 hurt your chances, and I intend to last. I know why there is no glass, in front of the water-colour picture of blue irises, and why the window only opens partly and why the glass is shatterproof.

Task

Think about how this description of the setting of a room acts as more than a simple description of a place. In your marking up of this text, in addition to the usual observations, concentrate particularly on marking the words/phrases/ideas which you do not understand on your first reading.

Initial thoughts

There are several 'asides' from the actual description of the room – additions, comments of the narrator on her own description ...

For example:

- 'They've removed anything you could tie a rope to' (lines 3–4)
- ' – it only opens partly – ' (line 6)
- and the last sentence (lines 20–22).

This suggests some sort of suicide risk on the part of the inhabitant of the room.

So possibly it could be a mental hospital, or a prison, a barracks for conscripts ...

Don't make up your mind at this point.

Analysis

There are the four basic questions you have to try to answer:

Who? Here we have 'I'; 'Aunt Lydia'; (each of) 'us'; and 'they'.

'They' appear to be in opposition in some way to the narrator, or at least in a position of control – 'They've removed …' (line 3) 'the kind of touch they like' (line 10), 'flowers are still allowed' (line 14). There are also references to the government and the army.

'Aunt Lydia' – there doesn't appear to be much help with this.

'us' – there are more people (probably women) in the same position as she is – possibly 'Handmaids' – see title.

Where? In a modern western society? What clues can be used to give this idea?

'shatterproof glass' is modern (twentieth century); the rug is described as 'folk art, archaic, made by women' (line 10) suggesting (possibly) that a modern age appreciates these things which belong to the past.

When? Has already been touched on above. Often **When?** and **Where?** are intertwined.

What? The action described – the narrator is being confined in some way, as are some other women, and is not particularly happy with the idea. 'Why do I want?' (line 12)

'There's a lot that doesn't bear thinking about.' (line 19)

And now, the other two important questions:

Why? This should help us to work on the motivation/plot/central concerns. But in this short extract there does not appear to be enough information to help us at first reading.

How? From the use of detail, one gets the impression of a quite cool, calculating and strong personality: 'This is the kind of touch they like' (line 10) shows an understanding of the motives and tricks of 'they' – the opposition; 'I intend to last' (line 20) shows resolve; and 'I know why there is no glass …' (line 20) shows she is aware of the suicide risk which other women have to be defended against, but she is armoured against it by her knowledge.

The next step is to tackle the parts of the extract which you do not understand at first reading – or which require you to re-read and think.

For example:

1 'Waste not want not. I am not being wasted. Why do I want?' (line 12)
2 'Think of it as being in the army' (line 16).
3 'Nothing takes place in this bed but sleep; or no sleep.' (lines 17–18)
4 'Thinking can hurt your chances, and I intend to last.' (lines 19–20)

1 Notice that 'want' is being used here in the sense of 'lack' (of something) rather than 'desire' (for something). What is it she lacks – freedom, her past life, autonomy? There is not enough information to deduce what this is.

2 Is this some sort of 'service' which society requires of her? The comparison is probably important because the information is given to you in a separate one line paragraph.

3 The other important activity other than sleep is probably sex. So sex is not to take place in this bed – but why mention that? It could be important. The statement is immediately followed by 'There's a lot that doesn't bear thinking about.'

4 The suggestion is that there is something she is going to have to put up with which is unpleasant – unpleasant enough to make the sufferers think of suicide – so she is not going to dwell on it in case she goes mad.

If you now go back to your initial thoughts, it becomes unlikely that she is in a prison – possibly more of a 'service' of some kind – a Handmaid – but not voluntary.

A mental hospital seems unlikely too – she sounds quite sane and aware of her predicament and its dangers.

A barracks – it seems too comfortable – 'Sunlight comes in through … polish' (lines 8–9), almost as if she is being kept safe and comfortable so that she can better fulfil her function.

Summary

Ultimately the setting allows you to deduce that the narrator is being kept in comfortable confinement in order to fulfil some task which society is demanding of her, and of other women like her. That the task is so unpleasant that suicide must have been at some point, and by other people, preferred as an alternative. The other aspect which the reader has been led towards is that the society in which this happens is a very controlling one, and that possibly one of the central concerns of the novel to follow might be about power and control. This last thought begins to answer some of the 'Why' question which we left unanswered above.

Setting: creative writing

Having studied this setting, and the questions/answers it throws up, the next task is for you to make your own attempt to create a setting with some meaningful purpose.

Then, you should apply the same skills of analysis to your own (or your fellow students') work by editing.

Too many adjectives

The ~~towering, coal black,~~ iron gates rose up in front of me, as I stepped down onto the ~~lush,~~ mossy ground. It spread out like a carpet and ~~dotted~~ around amongst my feet, worn ~~and weathered~~ from the salt spray and decades of easterly winds, were the ~~decaying~~ weathered gravestones. They were coloured yellow and grey, covered with coarse lichen~~, which felt like sand paper to touch~~. Looming high into the clouds were the crumbling ruins of the cathedral, seagulls were circling through its barren windows, ~~perched on the tower top~~. As I stepped out of the sunlight and through the narrow ~~stone grey~~ archway, my eyes were drawn to the shimmering expanse in front of me; the sea. At the bottom of the hill lay the cobbled stone harbour. A warm blanket of golden sand wrapped around the mouth of it like a welcoming hug to the returning vessels.

- 'Towering' not needed
- Weathered is not needed with 'worn' but is better than 'decaying'
- 'Narrow' is the best of three – to contrast in size with 'expanse'
- The image in the last lines could be good – depends on what happens next
- Other words in green not quite right – either cut or replace

What happens next? Possibly some disaster – graves and 'safe' harbour?

The need for careful observation of detail

The oldest residents of the house were the spiders. Throughout many years they had weaved their webs between the thin spindles of the stair bannisters ~~and from the damp stained ceiling to the cracked walls of the room~~. It had been four decades since a footstep had echoed within these walls, since the dust ~~that lay over every surface like snow~~ had been disturbed. The only furniture was a ~~vintage/~~oak table ~~carved of oak~~ and upon it lay old tea cups ~~thickly encrusted with dried up mould~~. The only light source was the sun bursting through the gaps in the boarded up windows ~~and from the small gaps in the heavy velvet curtains~~. All around were the artefacts of a life lived and abandoned, mattresses, dolls, sepia photographs ... The smell of mildew lingered in the air and absolute silence ~~was heard~~/reigned ~~throughout, all except the creak of the wooden door as I stepped into this grim and gloomy building~~.

- Webs on bannisters better than ceiling/wall
- Snow simile not good (not enough point of comparison between dust/snow)
- Cups description is over the top
- Light source *either* shutters *or* curtains, not both
- 'was heard' – better to use an active verb 'reigned'
- Last section: observer is already *in* the building

What happens next? Possibly a flashback to the life of the previous family?

Narrative voice

In the first three examples which follow (A–C), the first-person narrators illustrate a variety of ways in which narrators can be unreliable – or less than reliable – about the events they are recounting. Example D is an example of the use of the framing device, and deals with two first-person narrators. Examples E and F are aspects of 'authorial voice/tone'. Example G is again first-person, but represents the 'stream of consciousness' school of writing.

A: One Flew Over The Cuckoo's Nest

Ken Kesey (1962)

This is the opening of the novel which is set in a mental institution. The narrator is a half Indian inmate, known as Chief Bromden.

> They're out there.
>
> Black boys in white suits up before me to commit sex acts in the hall and get it mopped up before I can catch them.
>
> They're mopping when I come out of the dorm, all three of them sulky and hating
> 5   everything, the time of day, the place they're at here, the people they got to work around. When they hate like this, better if they don't see me. I creep along the wall quiet as dust in my canvas shoes, but they got special sensitive equipment detects my fear and they all look up, all three at once, eyes glittering out of black faces like the hard glitter of radio tubes out of the back of an old radio.
>
> 10   'Here's the Chief. The *soo*-pah Chief, fellas. Ol'Chief Broom. Here you go, Chief Broom …'
>
> Stick a mop in my hand and motion me to the spot they aim for me to clean today, and I go. One swats the back of my legs with a broom handle to hurry me past.
>
> 'Haw, you look at 'im shag* it? Big enough to eat apples off my head an' he mind me like a baby.'
>
> 15   They laugh and then I hear them mumbling behind me, heads close together. Hum of black machinery, humming hate and death and other hospital secrets. They don't bother not talking loud about their hate secrets when I'm nearby because they think I'm deaf and dumb. Everybody think so. I'm cagey enough to fool them that much. If my being half Indian ever helped me in any way in this dirty life, it helped me being cagey, helped me all
> 20   these years.
>
> I'm mopping near the ward door when a key hits it from the other side and I know it's Big Nurse by the way the lock works cleave to the key, soft and swift and familiar she been around locks so long. She slides through the door with a gust of cold and locks the door behind her and I see her fingers trail across the polished steel – tip of each finger the same
> 25   color as her lips. Funny orange. Like the tip of a soldering iron. Color so hot or so cold if she touches you with it you can't tell which.
>
> *used here in the sense of 'get going/grab'

Task

In what ways might the first-person narrator here be considered both unreliable and reliable?

Analysis

We can approach this extract in the same way as the passages we have looked at in previous sections, but we are going to concentrate on how the reliability of the narrator affects what we can 'believe' or what we have to be 'suspicious of'.

It quite quickly becomes obvious that the narrator has a strange view of himself and the personnel in the ward – his view in the first paragraph is particularly warped. He sees himself at the centre of some large conspiracy where he must avoid being noticed in case he brings its power down on him – 'better they don't see me'.

He tries to avoid the notice of the 'Black boys in white suits' by 'creep(ing) along the wall quiet as dust in my canvas shoes' – which is obviously not a successful ploy – but he thinks that they notice him, not because they see him, but because they 'detect' him by the use of 'sensitive equipment'.

He tries to avoid drawing attention to himself by pretending to be deaf and dumb, and even sometimes by keeping his eyes closed.

Thus we are given a picture of someone who is 'mad' – some kind of paranoid disorder perhaps? Therefore we question the reliability of his narrative.

But we have to ask ourselves why the writer has chosen such a character as his narrator.

There are some clues even in this short extract. Chief says:

'Hum of black machinery, humming hate and death and other hospital secrets. They don't bother not talking loud about their hate secrets when I'm nearby because they think I'm deaf and dumb. Everybody think so.'

This means that we get 'privileged' information through him because it is thought by the other characters that he is in no danger of understanding or passing on any professional secrets/information.

He also, in a warped kind of way, has an understanding of character, shown in his description of Big Nurse. Although it is couched in very odd terms, we get the correct impression of her ways and attitudes throughout the novel:

'She slides through the door with a gust of cold … Color so hot or so cold if she touches you with it you can't tell which.'

She seems emotionless and cruel and unpredictable, which turns out to be the case.

In answer to the question, he is a more informed narrator than the other patients, and once we as readers have learned to draw the line between the paranoid and the true, he becomes in some ways a very reliable narrator.

B: The Remains of the Day

Kazuo Ishiguro (1989)

In the following extract the butler, Stevens, is reminiscing about his relationship in the past with the housekeeper of Darlington Hall, Miss Kenton.

5   News of the death had arrived some hours earlier; indeed, I had myself knocked on the door of her parlour that morning to hand her the letter. I had stepped inside for a brief moment to discuss some professional matter, and I recall we were seated at her table and in mid-conversation at the moment she opened the letter. She became very still, but to her credit she remained composed, reading the letter through at least twice. Then she put the letter carefully back in its envelope and looked across the table to me.

'It is from Mrs Johnson, a companion of my aunt. She says she died yesterday.' She paused a moment, then said: 'The funeral is to take place tomorrow. I wonder if it might be possible for me to take the day off.'

10   'I'm sure that could be arranged, Miss Kenton.'

'Thank you, Mr Stevens. Forgive me, but perhaps I may have a few moments alone.'

'Of course, Miss Kenton.'

I made my exit, and it was not until after I had done so that it occurred to me I had not actually offered her my condolences. I could well imagine the blow the news would be to
15   her, her aunt having been, to all intents and purposes, like a mother to her, and I paused out in the corridor, wondering if I should go back, knock and make good my omission. But then it occurred to me that if I were to do so, I might easily intrude upon her private grief. Indeed, it was not impossible that Miss Kenton, at that very moment, and only a few feet from me, was actually crying. The thought provoked a strange feeling to rise within me,
20   causing me to stand there hovering in the corridor for some moments. But eventually I judged it best to await another opportunity to express my sympathy and went on my way.

Consider the limits of the reliability of Mr Stevens as a narrator.

Task

Analysis

We have no reason to suspect that Stevens is not giving us a reliable account of the facts. But his ability to recount the emotional content of this scene seems to be very limited.

His language is very formal:

'News of the death'; 'I'm sure that can be arranged, Miss Kenton'; 'offered my condolences'; 'make good my omission'; etc.

The closest he gets to an expression of emotion is 'was actually crying' and, more importantly, 'The thought provoked a strange feeling to rise within me'. He seems to be so unacquainted with his own emotions that he can't understand that he feels real distress/disturbance/sympathy/affection …

As a narrator of fact then, he is totally reliable; but he is limited in his understanding of his own, and probably others', emotions. We, as readers, can see past his narrative into more subtle understanding of the state of relationships at Darlington Hall.

C: Enduring Love

Ian McEwan (1997)

These are the opening paragraphs of *Enduring Love* (1997), a novel by Ian McEwan. The first-person narrator is a scientist by training, now a scientific writer.

5

10

I'm holding back, delaying the information. I'm lingering in the prior moment because it was a time when other outcomes were still possible; the convergence of six figures in a flat green space has a comforting geometry from the buzzard's perspective, the knowable, limited plane of the snooker table. The initial conditions, the force, the direction of the force, define all consequent pathways, all angles of collision and return, and the glow of the overhead light bathes the field, the baize and all its moving bodies, in reassuring clarity. I think that while we were still converging, before we made contact, we were in a state of mathematical grace. I linger on our dispositions, the relative distances and the compass point – because as far as these occurrences were concerned, this was the last time I understood anything clearly at all.

15

What were we running towards? I don't think any of us would ever know fully. But superficially the answer was a balloon. Not the normal space that encloses a cartoon character's speech or thought, or, by analogy, the kind that's driven by mere hot air. It was an enormous balloon filled with helium, that elemental gas forged from hydrogen in the nuclear furnace of the stars, first step along the way in the generation of multiplicity and variety of matter in the universe, including ourselves and all our thoughts.

20

We were running towards a catastrophe, which itself was a kind of furnace in whose heat identities and fates would buckle into new shapes. At the base of the balloon was a basket in which there was a boy, and by the basket, clinging to a rope, was a man in need of help.

Task

The first-person narrator is telling us he is unreliable. Mark up sentences or phrases which give this impression.

Analysis

Look at the imagery in the first paragraph, based on a snooker table. In the second paragraph, the imagery is of the cosmos and the creation of stars. The third paragraph uses the image of a furnace, heating and melting metal.

These three images are all based on scientific concepts. The first is like a force diagram seen from above (the buzzard's viewpoint) and marking the starting positions of all the players 'playing' in the impending catastrophe. The second is dealing with the balloon, but uses cosmological/creation imagery. The third uses the image of a furnace capable of melting elements (probably including the truth of the characters and their futures). These images all relate to his perception of himself as an unreliable narrator.

Do we end by actually believing in his narrative because he makes us aware of his shortcomings? In other words, do we trust in someone who is not telling the whole truth, but who tells us that this is the case? (There is something in common here with extract G on page 74.)

Note: Metafiction is a term which you may come across in your reading of criticism, or literary theory, or textual analysis in its more abstract forms.

Metafiction is specifically fiction about fiction, i.e. fiction which deliberately reflects upon itself. It can be a story containing another work of fiction within itself, or a novel where the narrator intentionally exposes him or herself as the author of the story and comments upon it. The next two examples, D and E, illustrate these ideas. There are, of course, many other forms used in modern fiction. Ian McEwan is a prime exponent of this sort of writing, and *Atonement* is a good example.

D: A Tradition of Eighteen Hundred and Four

Thomas Hardy (1882)

This example is of one first-person narrator framing the narrative of another first-person narrator. The extract consists of the beginning and the end of this short story, with a very brief summary of the events recounted in the middle of the tale.

The widely discussed possibility of an invasion of England through a Channel tunnel has more than once recalled old Solomon Selby's story to my mind.

The occasion on which I numbered myself among his audience was one evening when he was sitting in the yawning chimney-corner of the inn-kitchen, with some others
5   who had gathered there, and I entered for shelter from the rain. Withdrawing the stem of his pipe from the dental notch in which it habitually rested, he leaned back in the recess behind him and smiled into the fire. The smile was neither mirthful nor sad, not precisely humorous nor altogether thoughtful. We who knew him recognized it in a moment: it was his *narrative* smile. Breaking off our few desultory remarks we drew up
10   closer, and he thus began:-

'My father, as you mid know, was a shepherd all his life, and lived out by the Cove four miles yonder. Of all the years of my growing up the ones that bide clearest in my mind were eighteen hundred and three, four, and five. This was for two reasons: I had just then grown to an age where a child's eyes and ears take in and note down everything
15   about him, and there was more at that date to bear in mind than there ever has been since with me. It was, as I need hardly tell ye, the time after the first peace, when Bonaparte was scheming his descent upon England. He had crossed the great Alp mountains, fought in Egypt, drubbed the Turks, the Austrians, and the Proosians, and now he thought he'd have a slap at us.

20   *He then tells of an encounter where he, while watching the sheep by night, with his Uncle Job, saw Napoleon himself with two officers and a map reconnoitering the beach in Dorset for a possible invasion fleet.*

When they were over the brow, we crope out, and went some little way to look after them. Halfway down they were joined by two others, and six or seven minutes took
25   them to the shore. Then from behind a rock, a boat came out into the weak moonlight of the Cove, and they jumped in; it put off instantly, and vanished in a few minutes between the two rocks that stand at the mouth of the Cove as we all know. We climmed back to where we had been before, and I could see, a short way out, a larger vessel, though still not very large. The little boat drew up alongside, was made fast to the stern
30   as I suppose, for the largest sailed away, and we saw no more.

My Uncle Job told his officers as soon as he got back to camp; but what they thought of it I never heard – neither did he. Boney's army never came, and a good job for me; for the Cove below my father's house was where he meant to land, as this secret visit showed. We coast-folk should have been cut down one and all, and I should not have sat here to tell this tale.'

35 We who listened to old Selby that night have been familiar with his simple grave-stone for these ten years past. Thanks to the incredulity of this age his tale has been seldom repeated. But if anything short of the direct testimony of his own eyes could persuade an auditor that Bonaparte had examined these shores for himself with a view to a practicable landing place, it would have been Solomon Selby's manner of narrating the
40 adventure which befell him on the down.

Christmas 1882

Note: The more you know about the history of the Napoleonic wars which culminated in Napoleon's defeat at Waterloo, the more you will be in a position to judge the answers. (Your own general knowledge – its scope and diversity – can increase your appreciation of much of your reading.)

Think about this double narrative.

1 Is Solomon Selby a reliable narrator? Is his narrative about Napoleon landing in Dorset in 1804 true?
2 Is the framing narrator aware, or unaware, of the truth of Selby's narrative? Is he, the framing narrator, himself reliable?

The answer to both of these questions is 'No'.

Find the evidence of the double unreliability.

E: Vanity Fair

W.M. Thackery (1847)

This extract is very near the beginning of the novel.

'Revenge may be wicked, but it's natural,' answered Miss Rebecca. 'I'm no angel.' And, to say the truth, she certainly was not.

For it may be remarked in the course of the previous conversation (which took place as the coach rolled along lazily by the river side) that though Miss Rebecca Sharp has
5 twice had occasion to thank Heaven, it has been, in the first place, for ridding her of some person whom she hated, and secondly, for enabling her to bring her enemies to some sort of perplexity or confusion; neither of which are very amiable motives for religious gratitude, or such as would be put forward by persons of a kind and placable disposition. Miss Rebecca was not, then, in the least kind or placable. All the world used
10 her ill, said this young misanthropist, and we may be pretty certain that persons whom all the world treats ill, deserve entirely the treatment they get. The world is a looking-glass, and gives back to every man the reflection of his own face. Frown at it, and it will in turn look sourly upon you; laugh at it and with it, and it is a jolly kind companion; and so let all young persons take their choice.

Analysis

Sometimes, as in this novel, the 'Authorial Voice' tells us directly what to think of a character's behaviour, and takes us into his confidence – 'And, to say the truth, she certainly was not.' and 'We may be pretty certain.'

The narrator here is telling us what to think of Becky Sharp, and we tend to be led by him; but again the narrator is not really reliable or unreliable; he is a reporter, but a reporter with an axe to grind, and we must be aware of that. It has been said of the narrator of *Vanity Fair* that 'he becomes one more character, different in kind and in function from the other characters, certainly, but a character nonetheless.'

F: Dombey and Son *(pages 49–52)*

As we have already seen, the narrator in this novel is neither reliable, nor unreliable, but he is giving the reader a slight 'angle' or prism through which we view Mr Dombey.

G: Molloy

Samuel Beckett (1951)

This example focuses on stream of consciousness narrative (sometimes known as interior monologue). This extract from the beginning of the novel introduces Molloy, the narrator of the book.

> It seems to me sometimes that I even knew my son, that I helped him. Then I tell myself it's impossible. It's impossible I could ever have helped anyone. I've forgotten how to spell too, and half the words. That doesn't matter apparently. Good. He's a queer one the one who comes to see me. He comes every Sunday apparently. The other days he isn't free. He's
> 5 always thirsty. It was he who told me I had begun all wrong, that I should have begun differently. He must be right. I began at the beginning, like an old ballocks, can you imagine that? Here's my beginning. Because they're keeping it apparently. I took a lot of trouble with it. Here it is. It gave me a lot of trouble. It was the beginning, do you understand? Whereas now it's nearly the end. Is what I do now any better? I don't know. That's beside the point.
> 10 Here's my beginning. It must mean something, or they wouldn't keep it. Here it is.
>
> This time, then once more I think, then perhaps a last time, then I think it'll be all over, with that world too. Premonition of the last but one but one. All grows dim.

Analysis

In this kind of writing, the words follow the often chaotic thoughts of the narrator – jumping from subject to subject in the way that our own thoughts do. The general effect is of reliability on the part of the narrator, because he 'seems' not to understand his own predicament, and so we believe him. But it is difficult to find a 'truth' or any certainty. The writer manipulates the narration/narrator for his own purposes.

The subject flits from seemingly random thought to the next 'connection': son; words and spelling; an obscure critical visitor; beginning at the beginning – possibly some work of art/literature? Certainly for both narrator and reader 'all grows dim' – but we tend to believe him.

Note: There are many other variant examples of narration in modernist, post-modernist, existentialist, magical-realist works in the literature of the twentieth and twenty-first centuries which are not covered in this book, but which provide fascinating scope for further study.

PROSE NON-FICTION

Introduction

The following passages from non-fiction – some complete essays, some extracts from longer works – provide opportunities for the study of specific techniques of non-fiction and develop some of the skills you need to approach its analysis.

As already demonstrated in the other sections of this book, the basic approach which works for all these passages is reading with concentration and noting or 'marking up' what seem to you to be the important areas/sentences/phrases/words even, which help you to understand the content, and appreciate the techniques the writer uses.

Another useful approach to textual analysis is to see it as a complement to, in this case, reflective writing. The two skills work well together. You may be a better critic than writer. Or your writing skills may be better than your analytical ones. Being able to do a bit of both is good advice.

> I have a mind myself and recognize
> Mind when I meet it in any guise
> No one can know how glad I am to find
> On any sheet the least display of mind.
>
> *Robert Frost*

Textual analysis is about two minds meeting on a page – the writer's and the reader's. This section is about making the most of the 'meeting of the minds' that occurs in any type of non-fictional writing.

Textual analysis of non-fiction should be the skill that is familiar to you after years of reading: essays; book, film and television reviews; political diatribes; biography and autobiography; travel writing; memoirs; scientific papers; historical theses ... the genre list seems endless ...

In earlier studies you have become familiar with techniques such as word choice, imagery, sentence structures, tone and mood, point of view, the effects of listing, paragraphing, punctuating ... the list of 'techniques' also seems endless ...

Several non-fiction 'essays' are presented to give you practice. You will find notes for these pieces which will help you to analyse and evaluate the success of this 'meeting of the minds'.

Since imitation is an excellent way to learn to write and also to appreciate the writing of others, it is worthwhile trying to use creative writing (reflective writing can be called 'creative') to help to appreciate what you observe in the writing of other authors. The writing activities will give you the opportunity to try using some of the techniques in your own writing.

A variety of writing forms or **genres** come under the heading of 'non-fiction'. Some of the important ones are:

- Travel writing
- Autobiography/biography
- Landscape/nature writing

These divisions should be helpful, but not worrying. An autobiographical piece about travelling to France or America by a young man with strong views on the politics of the times can tick many boxes. Trying to put a definitive genre label on what you read in non-fiction is not as important as using the form as a key to help you to appreciate the central concerns of the writing and to account for the effectiveness of the author's style.

You will use the techniques that you are becoming familiar with to analyse non-fiction – structure, persona, tone, mood, use of language and detail. Some of these keys will be more important than others in analysing these extracts. Work out which ones are most useful in helping you to appreciate the particular piece that you are reading.

Travel writing: structure of an essay

On a first reading of a piece of non-fiction, try to follow the writer's train of thought – a meeting of minds. Often the structure becomes fairly obvious early on in an essay, particularly in a piece of autobiography or biography where the structure may be chronological. It is a common way of reflecting upon past experience.

- Who is writing?
- What happens in the extract?
- Is there a series of events?
- Where does it take place or what are the circumstances?
- Is there an end? Or a realisation of some sort? A climax to an experience?

Read the autobiographical piece on the following pages which is an example of this type of writing where one event follows another in a time sequence. More is gradually revealed about the author.

A: Footsteps

Richard Holmes (1985)

In this piece of autobiographical writing *Footsteps*, the writer Richard Holmes is reflecting on a journey he made when he was eighteen in the Massif Central of France, during which he kept a travel diary. He wanted to follow in the footsteps of Robert Louis Stevenson who made the same journey in 1878. Read the extract below and mark up the extract, making some notes on the ideas and the techniques. After you have finished your notes, look at the ones at the end of the extract and compare them with your own.

> All that night I heard footsteps: down by the river through the dark trees, or up on the moonlit road from Le Puy to Le Monastier. But I saw nothing except the stars, hanging over me where I wanted to be, with my head on a rucksack, and my rucksack on the grass, lying alone somewhere in the Massif Central of France, dreaming of the dead
> 5   coming back to life again. I was eighteen.
>
> I had started a travel-diary, teaching myself to write, and trying to find out what was happening to me, what I was feeling. I kept it simple:
>
> Found a wide soft dry ditch under thorn hedge between the track and the little Loire.

Here lit candle once more, studied ground for red ants, then set out bed-roll with all
10   spare clothes between me and my waterproof cloak-sheet. Soon I was gazing up at
stars, thinking of all the beats and tramps and travellers *a la belle étoile* from RLS to JK.
Story of snakes that are drawn to body-heat and slide into your sleeping-bag. Cicadas
and strange sounds a river makes at night flowing over rocks. Slept fitfully but without
disturbance from man or beast, except a spider in my ear. Saw a green glow-worm like
15   a spark.

I woke at 5 a.m. in a glowing mist, my green sleeping-bag blackened with the dew, for the
whole plateau of the Velay is above two thousand feet. I made a fire with twigs gathered
the night before and set water to boil for coffee, in a *petit pois* tin with wire twisted round
it as a handle. Then I went down to the Loire, here little more than a stream, and sat
20   naked in a pool cleaning my teeth. Behind me the sun came out and the woodier smoke
turned blue. I felt rapturous and slightly mad.

I reached Le Monastier two hours later, in the local grocer's van, one of the square
Citroëns like a corrugated garden privy, which smelt of camembert and apples. Monsieur
Crèspy, chauffeur and patron, examined my pack and soaking bag as we jounced along
25   through rolling uplands. Our conversation took place in a sort of no-man's-land of
irregular French. M. Crèspy's patois and Midi twang battled for meaning against my
stonewall classroom phrases. After initial skirmishing, he adopted a firm line of attack.

'You are walking on foot?' he said, leaning back into the depths of the van with one arm
and presenting me with a huge yellow pear.

30   'Yes, yes. I am searching for *un Ecossais*, a Scotsman, a writer, who walked on foot
through all this beautiful country.'

'He is a friend of yours? You have lost him?' enquired M. Crèspy with a little frown.

'No, no. Well … Yes. You see, I want to find him.' My chin streamed hopelessly with
pear juice.

35   M. Crèspy nodded encouragingly: 'The pear is good, *n'cest-ce pas?*'

'Yes, it is very good.'

The Citroën lurched round a bend and plunged down towards a rocky valley, broken with
trees and scattered stone farmhouses, with pink tiled roofs and goats tethered in small
bright pastures where the sun struck and steamed. The spire of a church, perched on the
40   far hillside, pointed the horizon.

'There is Le Monastier. Look! Perhaps your friend is waiting for you,' said M. Crèspy with
great confidence.

'No, no, I don't think so,' I said. But it was exactly what I hoped.

I rummaged in my rucksack. 'You see, here is his book. It tells the story of his walk
45   on foot.'

M. Crèspy peered at the little brown volume, and the Citroën swung back and forth
across the road, the sound of rolling fruit growing thunderous behind us. I hastily
propped the book up on the dashboard, being careful not to cover the St Christophe
medal or the picture of Our Lady mounted above a cone of paper flowers. I ran my →

50   finger down the sketch map on the title page: Le Monastier, Pradelles, Langogne, Notre Dame des Neiges, Montagne du Goulet, Pic de Finiels, Le Pont-de-Montvert, Florac, Gorges du Tarn, St Jean-du-Gard – to me already magic names, a litany of hills and rivers, with a lone figure striding along them, laughing beckoning, even mocking: follow! follow!

55   M. Crèspy considered the map, and then my face, then the map again, and changed gear with a reflective air. 'It is far, it is far.'

'Yes, I said, 'it is two hundred and twenty kilometres.'

M. Crèspy raised a finger from the steering wheel. 'And you, you are Scottish then?'

'No, no. I am English. My friend – that is to say, Mr Stevenson – was Scottish. He walked
60   on foot with a donkey. He slept *à la belle étoile*. He ...'

'Ah, *that*!' broke in M. Crèspy with a shout, taking both hands from the steering wheel, and striking his forehead. 'I understand, I understand! You are on the traces of Monsieur Robert Louis Steamson. Bravo, bravo!'

'Yes, yes. I am following his paces!'

65   We both laughed and the Citroën proceeded by divine guidance.

'I understand, I understand,' repeated M. Crèspy. And I believe he was the first person who ever did.

Initial thoughts

Structure

The structure of the piece is chronological with the author recounting events and feelings on his first night – 'that night' – which suggests its importance as the beginning his journey. There is a lot of atmospheric detail in the first paragraph that 'sets the scene' in time and place with an air of fearfulness or misgiving about the adventure. Pick out some of this detail in your marking up.

The final short sentence – 'I was eighteen' – emphasises his youth and perhaps naivety of this early journal.

Notice how the structure is established.

The first sentence after the travel diary entry – 'I woke at 5 a.m.' – confirms the chronological structure ... followed by the next paragraph – 'I reached Le Monastier two hours later ...'

The danger with this type of structure is that in the hands of an inexperienced writer, the pen can slip into simply recording events chronologically without any reflection or detail to give the writing 'life' or individuality.

Look at this passage again and mark up some more detailed notes on the 'voice' or persona of the speaker that emerges. Then compare your notes to the ones below.

→

Persona

You may have observed some or all of the following aspects.

There is a lot of detail that conveys the fearfulness/uncertainty of the author (lines 1–5):

- 'all that night I heard' suggests that the writer did not get much sleep
- it also makes the scene somewhat fearful – 'footsteps', 'dark trees'
- 'dreaming of the dead coming back to life again' – is puzzling at this stage
- extract from the travel diary explains a bit – are 'the dead' referring to Robert Louis Stevenson and John Keats, two writers who kept such travel diaries in their young years?
- details in diary further suggest discomfort of situation – a ditch, a thorn hedge, red ants followed by fear of snakes drawn to body heat, strange river sounds at night, a spider
- 'green glow-worm like a spark' – image emphasises surrounding darkness instead of just saying 'I woke at 5 a.m.'

Holmes also gives details of some of the discomfort (lines 16–21):

- a glowing mist, a sleeping bag blackened with dew – damp – followed by
- attempts to clean, eat and heat up with sun coming out and wood smoke turning blue
- final sentence of this paragraph is important because it gives his feelings at this stage – 'rapturous and slightly mad' – reminding us of his youth and exhilaration at probably this first venture on his own in a foreign country

In the next paragraphs (lines 22–40), Holmes records much more than just the arrival in Le Monastier two hours later – his destination for the day. His account of Monsieur Crèspy makes the account interesting and humorous with its details:

- a local grocer's van – you can picture the French Citroën like a 'corrugated garden privy'
- sensual details like smell of camembert and apples and taste of pear juice and feelings of being 'jounced along' the twisty road
- visual picture of rocky valley, scattered stone farmhouses with pink tiled roofs, tethered animals, spire of church pointed to horizon

The dialogue between the two people is an effective way to reveal a lot about the writer and his purpose in this journey (lines 28–67):

- description of conversation as a sort of a battle on no-man's land – between 'M. Crèspy's patois' and the writer's 'stonewall classroom phrases' in French leading to 'initial skirmishing'
- 'a firm line of attack' continues battlefield metaphor of French between them
- M. Crèspy only comes to understand the search for the 'friend' when he finds that he walked on foot with a donkey – 'Monsieur Robert Louis Steamson' – accompanied by an example of their confusing French/English – 'You are on the traces' – 'Yes, I am following his paces!'
- The final line of this opening suggests that the author is attempting to write about more here than just an event. There is reflection, an idea that he is pursuing:
- '"I understand," repeated M. Crèspy. And I believe he was the first person who ever did.'

We should be intrigued. What is the idea?

Analysis

This is an effective opening to a piece of autobiographical travel writing for a number of reasons:

Structure

While the structure is uncomplicated – chronological, sequential – the writing is not driven by the narrative which would simply be 'first … and then … and then … finally'. This is because the writer has included details and description which help the reader to picture the scene. He also builds to a final, somewhat enigmatic statement – 'And I believe he was the first person who ever did [understand].'

Persona

A strong sense of the author emerges during the course of the extract: his youthfulness; his openness to new experiences and to the people he meets; a sense of his naivety (this may be his first real journey from home); the sense that he is 'on a mission' or has a goal; and his reliability and thoroughness as an observer.

Dialogue and character

He has also brought in dialogue and character in his journey along the road. M. Crèspy is vividly depicted and brought to life in his dialogue. Monsieur 'Steamson' is in the background.

Reflection

Finally, and probably most importantly, there is an idea here: reflection, thought, a central concern that has to do with the writer's youth, this probable first journey from home in a foreign country, a solo venture, his search for a writer from the past – all summed up in the final intriguing lines:

'"I understand, I understand," repeated M. Crèspy. And I believe he was the first person who ever did.'

This suggests that no one else – probably not even the writer himself at this stage – is completely sure about why he is undertaking this unusual journey. This is an effective way of making this an intriguing passage. The reader wants to know more …

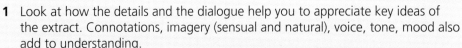

Tasks

1   Look at how the details and the dialogue help you to appreciate key ideas of the extract. Connotations, imagery (sensual and natural), voice, tone, mood also add to understanding.
2   The next extract is a continuation of the one above. After reading carefully and marking up your notes, go on to write a critical analysis of the extract.
    Drawing upon your knowledge of techniques, explain how the writer's style helps you to understand and appreciate the ideas.

Footsteps ... continued

After ten years of English boarding schools, brought up by Roman Catholic monks, I was desperate to slip the leash. Free thought, free travel, free love was what I wanted. I suppose a foreign *affaire de coeur* would have been the best thing of all; and that, in a way, was what I got.

5   It did not immediately occur to me to wonder what Stevenson himself was doing in that remote little town 'in the French highlands'. I knew he wanted to be a writer, had published essays in the London reviews, but was still struggling to establish his independence from his family in Edinburgh. They had brought him up a strict Calvinist, an outlook which he had rejected; and they had wanted him to be an engineer. Instead 10 he had adopted the life of a literary bohemian, affected wide-brimmed hats and velvet jackets, and fled to France whenever he could.

Staying at the little hotel at Le Monastier that autumn, he made friends with the local doctor. He had decided to pursue the road south himself, but on foot, in the company of a donkey to carry his baggage. This voyage resulted in the little brown volume I now 15 carried as my bible – his *Travels with a Donkey in the Cévennes.*

At Le Monastier that morning, the question of Stevenson's donkey bulked large. Unloaded from the van, I was taken into the backroom of the *épicerie* and given breakfast by Madame Créspy.

'When Monsieur Steamson was here, they used to make lace,' she said, also using the 20 local pronunciation. 'But you will want your donkey, like him. You must go and see Le Docteur Ollier.'

Mlle Crèspy, who looked at me with dark dancing eyes, was deputed to take me to the doctor. 'It's no fun without the donkey,' she observed, prettily rolling the colloquial word *rigolo*, and seizing me by the hand. Mlle Crèspy was about nine.

25 Le Docteur, a tall patient man, ushered me into his surgery and poured me a yellow medicine, which turned out to be a liqueur. 'Of course, there is the question of the donkey. You will have to consult the Mayor. Everyone takes a donkey.'

'Everyone?'

'Mlle Singer took a donkey. She was lost in a storm on the Lozère. It is high up there. The 30 fire brigade from Bleymard went out to find her with lanterns.'

I accepted another yellow medicine. 'This was recently, Miss Singer?'

'Oh, yes, this was in 1949. You must pay attention to the vipers,' concluded Dr Ollier.

'So you desire to hire a donkey,' said the Mayor, as we paced in the cobbled courtyard of the old Bishop's palace.

35 I looked abashed. 'I am following Stevenson. But I have my sack.'

The Mayor reflected. 'You see, Monsieur Steamson, he had a donkey. It is in his book. It is *charming* for a writer to have a donkey. It is his companion of the route.'

The sun beat down, the liqueur rose in my head, I had a vague sense that things were getting out of hand even before I had started. The reality of Stevenson's presence in Le 40 Monastier was uncanny. I asserted myself rather desperately. 'No, no, I do not desire a donkey. My companion of the route – is Monsieur Stevenson himself!'

→

45   The Mayor stopped short, took off his small gold spectacles and tapped me on the chest. 'Of course, of course,' he said, beaming suddenly. 'You are young, indeed you are young, and I wish you a good journey with all my heart.' He replaced his spectacles and shook my hand many times, and I shook his quite as often. 'You know,' added the Mayor as we parted, 'Monsieur Steamson purchased his donkey for sixty-five francs. I could not easily find you such a bargain. But still, after all, if you should desire …'

Task

Write your own autobiographical account of a journey you made or a travel experience which you have had, perhaps solo. You may use a straightforward, chronological structure; however, the account must be more than narrative. There should be reflection on the experience which is made 'real' to the reader through the use of detail.

On your first draft it may help to highlight or underscore the places where you reflect upon the experience. (This ensures that you do *reflect* as well as *narrate*.)

Postcard from Rome, by the well-known journalist Clive James was one of a number of 'postcards' he sent home to readers on places of interest that he was commissioned to visit and to write about. Like *Footsteps*, it is travel writing; it is autobiographical; it has a structure; and, importantly, it is reflective.

B: Postcard from Rome

Clive James (1979)

Read the passage first and then, on a second reading, make notes on the structure and the tone James uses to present Rome to the reader. You should also highlight the places where he reflects upon his visit to Rome, upon thoughts and ideas that arise because of the experience.

British Airways were justifiably proud of getting your correspondent to Rome only three hours behind schedule. After all, Heathrow had been in the grip of those freak snow conditions which traditionally leave Britain stunned with surprise.

5   In England, British Rail loudspeakers had been smugly announcing prolonged delays due to locomotives coming into contact with inexplicable meteorological phenomena, such as heaps of water lying around in frozen form. Airport officials were equally flabbergasted to discover more of the same stuff falling out of the sky. But now my staunch Trident was leaving all that behind. In a dark but clear midnight, Rome lay below. Those strings of lights were roads all leading to the same place.

10   All my previous visits to the Eternal City had been done on the cheap. I used to live in the kind of cold-water *pensione* on the Via del Corso where the original rooms had been partitioned not only vertically but horizontally as well, so that the spiral staircase beside your bed led up to a bare ceiling. You had to apply in writing to take a bath. Lunch was half a plate of pasta on the other side of the Tiber. Dinner was the other half.

→

15   A lot of water has gone over the viaduct since then, and this time I was a *bona fide* traveller. Even at one o'clock in the morning Leonardo da Vinci airport, tastefully done out in fluted chromium, was a treat for the eyes. My hotel was in Piazza Trinita dei Monti at the very top of the Spanish Steps. The decor was strictly veneers and cut glass, but it was heavily tricked out with the Medici coat of arms and the bath came ready equipped

20   not just with a plug, but a dinky sachet of foam-producing green goo. My waiting readers were subsidising this luxury. Could I justify their confidence? What can you say about so old a city in so short a space? I sank cravenly into the foam.

Sleep allayed my fears, but they came back in the morning. I appeared on the Spanish Steps just in time to be greeted by the cold weather, which had been racing down

25   Europe during the night. Rome suddenly froze up solid. The Triton, forever blowing his conch in the Piazza Barberini, abruptly became festooned with icicles. As unashamedly ostentatious as ever, the wealthier Roman women shopping in the Via Condotti instantly adopted a uniform – mink and boots. In the bar a little fat lady who looked like a bale of furs reached up to spoon the cream from a glass of hot chocolate higher than her head.

30   For once nobody was in any danger of being kidnapped. Cold weather meant plenty of snow in the mountain resorts. The terrorists were all away skiing.

With only a few days at my disposal I decided to leave most of the usual haunts unvisited. I headed out by car to the Catacombs, where a German monk took me down into the ground. 'Zer soil is called tufa. Volcanig. Easy for tunnels. Mind zer head.'

35   In this one set of catacombs there are eleven miles of tunnels, one network under another. The two top levels have electric light throughout. 'Mine apologies for zer electric light. Mit candles is more eerie. Zis way.' People had been filed away down here by the generation. Some of the frescos remain intelligible. You can see the style changing through time: suddenly a Byzantine Christ tells you that the Empire of the

40   West is in decline. The sign of the fish is everywhere. 'You also see zer sign of zer turtle dove. Symbol of luff und piss.'

Everything and everywhere in and around Rome is saturated with time. If you look too long, you will be hypnotised. When Rome ceased to be the capital city of an international empire, it reverted to being a provincial town. Though it has been officially called so

45   since 1870, it has never really become the capital of Italy – not in the way London is the capital of England or Paris of France. Rome produces little. For a long time it has been a consumers' town. Even the Renaissance was produced in Florence and consumed in Rome. Bringing Michelangelo to Rome was like bringing Tolstoy to Hollywood.

Rome is a good place for madmen to dream of building empires. It is a bad place from

50   which to govern Italy. Mussolini chose the first option, with the inevitable consequences. The most recent of Rome's overlords, he left the fewest traces. Apart from the embarrassingly fine architecture of the EUR district out on the periphery, the city gives almost no indication that he ever lived. The Palazzo di Venezia is, of course, still there. You can pick out the balcony from which he shouted to the crowds and the window

55   behind which he left a light burning at night to encourage the notion that he never slept.

The reason that the Empire could never be restored was that the world grew out of it. The Roman Empire died of success. It was already dying when Scipio Africanus became the first Roman to take a bath as often as once a week. It was already dying when the legions in Sicily met their first Greeks and began learning the ways of cultivated leisure.

60   Livy's history is one long lament for the old Republic – a warning to Augustus that the tribe's disciplined impulse was on the wane.

65

But Livy never saw that he himself was part of the problem. Nor did Tacitus at a later time. The city which had once been little more than a base camp had become a civilisation. It was changing at the centre. The decline was really a transformation. The Empire became the church, which became other churches, which became the Enlightenment, which became the modern age. The centurions became the priests who became us. With the eyes history has given us, we can now see that to unite the world is no longer a sane aim. It has already become united, within the individual soul.

70

Meanwhile the city of Rome is left with nothing but its heritage. There is a lot to look after. Things get stolen, or just fall apart. In the Piazza Navona I found the Bernini fountains plump with ice, like overfilled tubs of lemon *gelato*. But it's unfair on Rome to let the weather get you down. In spring and summer the fountains ionise the air to the point that the third-rate expatriate American writers who infest the city feel themselves brimming over with creative energy. Yet even then you can detect the weariness beneath the fervour.

75

No less afraid of dying than anybody else, I still like the idea of what Lucretius describes as the reef of destruction to which all things must tend, *spatio aetatis defessa vetusto –* worn out by the ancient lapse of years. But I don't want to see the reef every day.

The Spanish Steps were a cataract. Climbing them like an exhausted salmon, I passed the window of the room in which Keats coughed out the last hours of his short life with

80

nothing to look at except a cemetery to time. No wonder he forgot his own vitality and declared that his name was writ in water. As he should have realised, the thing to do when you feel like that is to pack up and catch a plane to London. Which I did.

Initial thoughts

Point of view and tone

The opening two paragraphs (lines 1–9) establish the point of view – 'your correspondent' – and a humorous tone:

- 'only three hours behind schedule' – understatement in 'only'
- 'stunned with surprise' – personifies Britain with humour – 'stunned' at arrival of ice and snow
- anonymous personification 'smugly' and 'flabbergasted'
- humour in juxtaposition of technical language of 'inexplicable meteorological phenomena' compared to colloquial phrase 'heaps of water lying around in frozen form' and 'stuff falling out of the sky'
- good image of approaching Rome in the dark with 'strings of lights' leading to centre

In paragraphs 3 and 4 (lines 10–22), details of an earlier visit to 'Eternal City' tell more about author and add to lighthearted tone:

- colloquial 'on the cheap'
- exaggeration of impoverished conditions with rooms partitioned vertically and horizontally, applying in writing to take a bath, lunch served miles away and other half of same meal served at night
- humour in 'A lot of water has gone over the viaduct' instead of 'under the bridge' in keeping with Roman landscape
- exaggeration of airport decoration of 'fluted chromium', 'a treat for the eyes', 'strictly veneers and cut glass' – artificial and cheap
- finished with a bath, not only with a plug but also 'green goo'
- 'my waiting readers subsidising this luxury'
- rhetorical questions 'Could I justify ...'
- climax at end of paragraph 'I sank cravenly into the foam'

In paragraph 5 (lines 23–31), details of events next day continue with the same humorous tone:

- description of cold weather evidenced on Spanish Steps – setting scene
- Triton blowing conch 'festooned with icicles'
- uniform of wealthy Roman women in mink and boots
- exaggeration of little fat lady like a 'bale of furs' trying to reach to the top of her hot chocolate
- final line – terrorists were all away skiing

In paragraph 6 (lines 32–41), dialogue of German monk is effective in describing Catacombs with humour:

- imitations of his accent – e.g. 'luff and piss'

Reflection

In paragraphs 7 and 8 (lines 42–55), James reflects on a number of ideas connected with Rome:

- Rome – 'saturated with time'
- Rome – a small place and not a capital like London or Paris
- a consumer town – not a producer
- Rome – a place to rule from – a place for 'madmen to dream of building empires' but not for governing

In paragraphs 9 and 10 (lines 56–68), he begins to reflect on the death of Rome:

- end of Empire – was because of its success. Rome changed from a base camp to a civilisation – its decline was a transformation with Empire becoming a Church becoming other churches, becoming Enlightenment and then the modern age
- Climax of 'postcard' in world 'has already become united, within the individual soul' – puzzle to ponder? Paradox

Structure

Paragraphs 11 and 12 (lines 69–82) form the conclusion:

- back to weather (from beginning)
- back to Spanish Steps
- good image of James climbing them like 'exhausted salmon' trying to climb the ladder in a river to return to place of birth to breed
- image of Keats 'coughing out last hours', saying that his life was transient – 'writ in water'
- back to London finally
- short final sentence in catching a plane back to London – 'Which I did.'

Analysis

At the very beginning, he establishes a relationship with his readership with a **tone** that is informal, entertaining, but also informative and reflective. Although the piece is light-hearted in many ways, it is not without reflection and it should give the reader ideas to think about.

You may have commented in your notes that there is a clear **structure** to this piece of travel writing. The author establishes his arrival from snow-swept England to Rome in an effective way and reflects on his earlier acquaintance with the Eternal City. The cold weather sweeps into Rome from the north the next day and influences his description of the inhabitants, as well as the sites he visits and tries to bring alive for his readers.

In terms of structure, he brings the piece to a very neat end, even coming back to the Spanish Steps, following the same pattern as the opening with comments on the adverse weather, his thoughts about Rome on this visit, and the final departure for London. This return to the ideas and pattern of the beginning makes for a satisfying rounding off, or conclusion.

Within the piece, he selects certain features to visit and to reflect upon. As well as moving about sites in Rome, he is also moving back through the centuries to discuss events and his feelings about the past. The idea of time or transience runs throughout this passage.

Although there is humour throughout the piece, this reflective piece of travel writing is thought-provoking and raises ideas and questions for readers to consider:

- Rome – a capital city but not in the way that Paris and London are capitals?
- Rome – a good place for mad empire-builders to dream but a bad place to govern?
- Rome – civilisation grew out of Rome and the Empire died of that success?

Finally, is there a thread that runs throughout? The brevity of individual lives? The transience of individual existence (Keats?) 'The reef of destruction to which all things must end'? A depressing thought or a necessary recognition? 'I don't want to see the reef every day', James concludes, and catches the plane back to London.

Task

You have read two pieces of travel writing which are different, but both have the essential ingredient of *reflection*: presentation of ideas for the reader's consideration – a meeting of minds on the page.

They also both have a clear, fairly straightforward *structure* in establishing person, place, time and point of view at the beginning and concluding by returning, in some specific detail, to the person, place, time and point of view at the end. There is a satisfying rounding off for the reader, a feeling that the writer is in charge of the journey that he has taken you on during the course of the passage.

A sense of the writer or *persona* emerges from both of these essays in the *tone* which makes the writing engaging for the reader.

After you are satisfied that you have considered the effects of both of these essays in detail, try writing another piece of your own travel writing or revising the piece that you have already written, having acquired more insight into effective reflective writing.

As you plan the essay and begin to write or to revise, remember to give some attention to:

- reflecting upon the experience
- structuring the essay (perhaps returning at the end to ideas introduced at the beginning)
- establishing a relationship with the reader through the tone you use
- employing techniques that develop character and setting, or whatever is appropriate to your content and style.

Autobiography: persona and tone

In some essays, the sense of the writer is clearer than in others because of the voice or tone which the writer uses. Casual, colloquial, informal writing styles can make the reader feel as if he is having a conversation with the writer in which he is getting to know him. In this type of writing, understanding and appreciating the tone and the way the author is developing it, is of particular importance in textual analysis.

The following extract gives you the opportunity to analyse the ways in which a writer uses tone, as well as other techniques, to reflect on personal experience and to develop ideas. Good non-fiction writing often leaves the reader thinking, 'I know what he means'; in other words, the universal experience is conveyed through the individual or personal details.

Autobiography

Mark Twain (written between 1877 and 1904)

Read the following extract which reflects upon a writer's origins and his sources for writing. Twain is the American author of *The Adventures of Tom Sawyer* (1876) and *The Adventures of Huckleberry Finn* (1884). The period he is writing about is before the abolition of slavery in 1865. As you read the passage, pay particular attention to the persona and the tone used.

I was born the 30th of November, 1835, in the almost invisible village of Florida, Monroe County, Missouri. My parents removed to Missouri in the early thirties; I do not remember just when, for I was not born then and cared nothing for such things. It was a long journey in those days and must have been a rough and tiresome one. The village
5   contained a hundred people and I increased the population by 1 percent. It is more than many of the best men in history could have done for a town. It may not be modest in me to refer to this but it is true. There is no record of a person doing as much – not even Shakespeare. But I did it for Florida and it shows that I could have done it for any place – even London, I suppose.

10   Recently some one in Missouri has sent me a picture of the house I was born in. Heretofore I have always stated that it was a palace but I shall be more guarded now.

The village had two streets, each a couple of hundred yards long; the rest of the avenues mere lanes, with rail fences and cornfields on either side. Both the streets and the lanes were paved with the same material – tough black mud in wet times, deep dust in dry.

15   My uncle, John A Quarles, was a shopkeeper and also a farmer, and his place was in the country four miles from Florida. He had eight children and fifteen or twenty negroes and was also fortunate in other ways, particularly in his character. I have not come across a better man than he was. I was his guest for two or three months every year, from the fourth year after we removed to Hannibal till I was eleven or twelve years old. I have
20   never consciously used him or his wife in a book but his farm has come very handy to me in literature once or twice. In *Huck Finn* and in *Tom Sawyer, Detective* I moved it down to Arkansas. It was all of six hundred miles but it was no trouble; it was not a very large farm – five hundred acres, perhaps – but I could have done it if it had been twice as large. And as for the morality of it, I cared nothing for that; I would move a state if the
25   exigencies of literature required it.

30 The farmhouse stood in the middle of a very large yard and the yard was fenced on three
sides with rails and on the rear side with high palings; against these stood the smoke-
house; beyond the palings was the orchard; beyond the orchard were the negro quarters
and the tobacco fields. The front yard was entered over a stile made of sawed-off logs
of graduated heights; I do not remember any gate. In a corner of the front yard were a
dozen lofty hickory trees and a dozen black walnuts, and in the nutting season riches
were to be gathered there.

Down a piece, abreast the house, stood a little log cabin against the rail fence; and
there the woody hill fell sharply away, past the barns, the corn-crib, the stables and
35 the tobacco-curing house, to a limpid brook which sang along over its gravelly bed
and curved and frisked in and out and here and there and yonder in the deep shade of
overhanging foliage and vines – a divine place for wading, and it had swimming pools,
too, which were forbidden to use and therefore much frequented by us. For we were little
Christian children and had early been taught the value of forbidden fruit.

40 All the negroes were friends of ours, and with those of our own age we were in effect
comrades. I say in effect, using the phrase as a modification. We were comrades and yet
not comrades; colour and condition interposed a subtle line which both parties were
conscious of and which rendered complete fusion impossible. We had a faithful and
affectionate good friend, ally and adviser in 'Uncle Dan'l', a middle-aged slave whose
45 head was the best one in the negro quarter, whose sympathies were wide and warm and
whose heart was honest and simple and knew no guile. He has served me well these
many, many years. I have not seen him for more than half a century and yet spiritually
I have had his welcome company a good part of that time and have staged him in
books under his own name and as 'Jim', and carted him all around – to Hannibal, down
50 the Mississippi on a raft and even across the Desert of Sahara in a balloon and he has
endured it all with the patience and friendliness and loyalty which were his birthright.
It was on the farm that I got my strong liking for his race and my appreciation of certain
of its fine qualities. This feeling and this estimate have stood the test of sixty years and
more and have suffered no impairment. The black face is as welcome to me now as it
55 was then.

In my schoolboy days I had no aversion to slavery. I was not aware that there was
anything wrong about it. No one arraigned it in my hearing; the local papers said nothing
against it; the local pulpit taught us that God approved it, that it was a holy thing and
that the doubter need only look in the Bible if he wished to settle his mind – and then the
60 texts were read aloud to us to make the matter sure; if the slaves themselves had an
aversion to slavery they were wise and said nothing. In Hannibal we seldom saw a slave
misused; on the farm never.

There was, however, one small incident of my boyhood days which touched this matter,
and it must have meant a good deal to me or it would not have stayed in my memory,
65 clear and sharp, vivid and shadowless, all these slow-drifting years. We had a little slave
boy whom we had hired from some one, there in Hannibal. He was from the eastern shore
of Maryland and had been brought away from his family and his friends halfway across
the American continent and sold. He was a cheery spirit, innocent and gentle, and the
noisiest creature that ever was, perhaps. All day long he was singing, whistling, yelling,
70 whooping, laughing – it was maddening, devastating, unendurable. At last, one day, I lost
all my temper and went raging to my mother and said Sandy had been singing for an
hour without a single break and I couldn't stand it and *wouldn't* she please shut him up.
The tears came into her eyes and her lip trembled and she said something like this:

'Poor thing, when he sings it shows that he is not remembering and that comforts me;
75   but when he is still I am afraid he is thinking and I cannot bear it. He will never see his
mother again; if he can sing I must not hinder it, but be thankful for it. If you were older
you would understand me; then that friendless child's noise would make you glad.'

It was a simple speech and made up of small words but it went home, and Sandy's noise
was not a trouble to me any more. She never used large words but she had a natural
80   gift for making small ones do effective work. She lived to reach the neighbourhood of
ninety years and was capable with her tongue to the last – especially when a meanness
or an injustice roused her spirit. She has come handy to me several times in my books,
where she figures as Tom Sawyer's Aunt Polly. I fitted her out with a dialect and tried
to think up other improvements for her but did not find any. I used Sandy once, also; it
85   was in *Tom Sawyer*. I tried to get him to whitewash the fence but it did not work. I do not
remember what name I called him by in the book.

Task

This piece of first-person writing is the opening to *The Autobiography of Mark Twain*
written in the nineteenth century. Twain reflects here upon his early life, growing up in
Missouri. At first reading it seems to be solely about himself; however, when you read carefully you see that it
is about the setting, the time and the place, as much as about his own life. He is also reflecting on a number
of different concerns.

Mark up the passage, noting particularly the places where you think his writing is about human experience
generally. Also notice how he is establishing a voice or tone, a relationship with the reader. You can
compare your notes to the ones which follow.

Initial thoughts

Twain's style of humour – almost a sense of absurdity – is apparent from the start of the passage when
he is talking about his beginnings:

By just being born, he managed to increase the population of Florida, his hometown, by one per cent.
This tongue-in-cheek humour continues throughout the passage, but this initial comment signals that
understatement, gentle irony, is going to be characteristic of the tone.

In paragraphs 2/3/4 (lines 10–25), there is a humorous way of saying that his beginnings were
humble:

- reinforced by the description of the village: 'tough black mud in wet times, deep dust in dry' and
houses made of logs
- humour in the absurdity of moving his uncle's farm and family if it helped his writing
- reflection in the idea of making things up in literature if required

In paragraphs 5/6 (lines 26–39), description of farmhouse and steading reinforces humble beginnings:

- 'negro quarters' is the first reminder that this piece was written during times of slavery in the
southern States
- humour in final line of the previous paragraph: 'we were little Christian children and had early
been taught the value of "forbidden fruit"' – humour produced from statement the opposite to
what you expect

In paragraph 7 (lines 40–55), he reflects on the idea that negroes were friends but comments on differences:

- 'We were comrades and yet not comrades' and subtle line between white and black
- second friend, Uncle Daniel, used in books – talks about him like in the way he spoke of the farm – 'carted him all around'
- absurdity and humour of statement – 'he endured it all with patience and friendliness'
- subtle reflection on racial differences summed up in final sentence of paragraph: 'The black face is as welcome to me now as it was then.'

In paragraph 8 (lines 56–62), he goes on to discuss slavery:

- reminder to us that it was a way of life in the South then when Twain was writing

Starting in paragraphs 9 and 10 (lines 63–77), poignant conclusion with story of small slave boy separated from family:

- gives his childish point of view – annoyance of the constant noise Sandy made
- his mother's reaction expressed meaningfully and succinctly – tears in her eyes, lips trembling
- her words as closely as he can remember – and memory of her simple language
- this is a subtle example of horror of slavery without Twain moralising or explaining about it

Concludes in final paragraph with appropriate picture of his mother (inspiration for Aunt Polly):

- 'I fitted her out with dialect and tried to think up other improvements for her'
- reference to whitewashing fence in Tom Sawyer
- final understatement – I do not remember what name I called him by in the book
- contrast to how vividly Twain remembers these people – his mother, Uncle Daniel and Sandy

Analysis

This opening passage to Twain's autobiography seems, at first, to be very simple and matter-of-fact. It is the tone which he uses, the humour produced from understatements and exaggerations and gentle irony that makes us aware that he is reflecting upon the sources for much of his writing. He is also reflecting upon a way of life in the South – not just his life – but generally.

His comments on using personal experience and childhood memories to enrich one's writings are reflective. He mentions – without discussing – the morality of exaggerating or, indeed, changing circumstances and facts to produce fiction. He does this with the farm, his uncle, Uncle Daniel, Sandy and his own mother. He is discussing, in a subtle way, the uses that a writer makes of his background and acquaintance in literature.

The fact that he does not actually discuss fully the concerns that he mentions, perhaps makes the reflection more provocative for the reader. This is very much the case when he is discussing slavery and the plight of black people pre-Civil War. He makes the discussion meaningful and even poignant by using people he knew: Uncle Daniel, Sandy and even his mother's relationship with the slaves. He never mentions the morality of slavery; in fact, there is no evidence even for making statements about his position on the issue. It is important to remember that this autobiography was written in different times – when slavery was a way of life. The fact that Twain has presented these people in his autobiography with these simple, but telling, incidents from his childhood suggest the importance that they must have had in his mind even then when slavery was the economic basis to the way of life in the Southern cotton and tobacco growing states. He states about the Sandy incident: 'it must have meant a good deal to me or it would not have stayed in my memory, clear and sharp, vivid and shadowless, all these slow-drifting years.'

Twain's style of writing makes us reflect upon the effectiveness of 'discussing' issues in an autobiographical way: presenting incidents and people without sermonising. Perhaps this is as effective a way to express ideas as giving strong opinions for or against an issue? The ways in which Twain presents and discusses slavery certainly make the people and the incidents referred to both memorable and poignant.

His colloquial style of writing, the way he would speak in a rambling sort of way, makes this opening to his autobiography seem like a friendly, introductory conversation with someone. It is in no way assertive, didactic or instructive.

Twain said that he wanted his autobiography to bring past and present together to 'fire up interest all along like contact of flint with steel'. He also did not want to select from his life … 'its showy episodes', but deal merely in the common experiences which go to make up the life of the average human being. The narrative must interest the average human being because these episodes are of a sort which he is familiar with in his own life and in which he sees his own life reflected and set down in print.

One of the best ways of appreciating the style of autobiography that Twain uses in this extract is, perhaps, to write an autobiographical piece of your own drawing upon a childhood memory of an incident or childhood memories generally. There is no reason to try to write in a similar way to Twain; develop your own style. The tone does not have to be humorous.

You may wish to compare your writing style with others in the class or with the one given here by another student. Write your own first before you look at any others, including the one that follows.

Reflective: creative writing

Twain said that he wanted his autobiography 'to fire up an interest all along like the contact of flint with steel'. He also did not want to select from his life 'its showy episodes', but rather to deal with the common experiences which make up the life of an average human being.

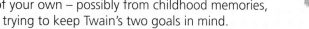

Write an autobiographical piece of your own – possibly from childhood memories, or from more recent experience – trying to keep Twain's two goals in mind.

When you have finished, ask yourself the following questions:

- Is there a clear reflection on one or two ideas arising from the incidents related?
- Is there a structure which shows control – an effort to present material effectively? Is it, for example, chronological, circular, climactic, parallel …?
- Does a persona or speaker emerge from the writing, probably through the adoption of a consistent tone (humorous/regretful/nostalgic/tragic …)?

The following autobiographical essay, written by a student, in a humorous style, has some serious reflective elements. After you have read it, compare it with your own writing in terms of structure, persona, tone, and style.

Heroes

As far back as I can remember (I am eighteen), I have always seen myself as a 'hero'. At four years of age I paraded the village neighbourhood where I live beating my bare chest (in the summer), yodelling as I swooped gracefully Tarzan-like from tree to tree. When I was five years old, people pointed in amazement and asked, 'Is it a bird? Is it a plane?' No, it was me as I darted super-fashion down our drive. That year I rid West Park Avenue of Indians. I continued to clean up the neighbourhood of demons and other scum like the English on Halloween as I took my village by storm in 1995, '96 and '97 as Ghostbuster, William Wallace and Robert the Bruce. My final performance as Robin Hood surpassed all others and wealth was redistributed (in my mind, at least) from … old to young.

I was not quite such a hero, however, when I had to have my hair cut. Legend has it that I had to be forcefully pinned down howling interminably. Hairdressers not only had never met a boy like me, but neither had they seen hair like mine. Even it was heroic: it curled thickly and stiffly like steel wool over my ears – before I was scalped by a female Indian in a blue pinny in the middle of our kitchen floor.

Once at the Grammar School, the days of my heroism and my howling haircuts seemed to be coming to an end. I tried my hand at playing pretend in the school drama club for a while, but after the starring roles to which I had become accustomed in the neighbourhood, I was uninspired by the ordinary nature of the parts I was given. I was destined for Greatness.

Just as I was beginning to feel mature (and had learned how to flatten my thicket of hair with water), Examinations – and Shakespeare – became my Fate. I did not read books about proper heroes any more, it seemed; I could not identify with the new 'heroes'. Instead I read and wrote essays about Shakespearean plays and 'character development'. At the age of thirteen, when it was still a slaggable offence to talk decently to girls, I found it difficult to relate to Lysander in *A Midsummer Night's Dream*. Themes about the blindness of love had little relevance for me at this point in my life. Puck seemed more a possibility – at least I liked his mischief and I could continue to throw my spitballs and to play the odd prank.

By second year, it was not such a cardinal sin to speak to girls. We read *The Merchant of Venice* which had appealing themes about justice and exacting a pound of flesh. Unfortunately, it was yet another Shakespearean play in which I could find no attractive hero. Antonio lost his worldly goods and seemed a bit wimpish. Shylock was no one's figure for the future. I could relate only to Portia, not something to be admitted at this time of one's life.

Romeo and Juliet seemed to come at an appropriate time in my life – fourteen. By this, I do not mean that I – or any of the other boys in my class – had been anywhere near the emotion of love, but rather that we were beginning to become aware that we had (or might someday have) hormones – mostly apparent in our facial skin conditions – but also in the form of (dare I say it?) 'lust'. Like Romeo with his feelings for the opposite sex, we all choked on love (or liked to imagine that we did). However, again I could not really see the 'hero' that I had once been in my tree-swinging days. I could relate to Romeo but I did not aspire to be him; certainly I did not see him as a hero. He did not seem the sort of lad who could throw a skilful reverse pass on the rugby pitch. And the idea of marriage, declaring undying love or chatting up girls to get a kiss with lines like 'Then move not while my prayer's effect I take' made me lose faith in this character.

Only in fourth year, did I, at last, finally, begin to find worthy recipients for my adulation. I could relate to the characters and ideas of *Macbeth* although he met a rather untimely end which I hoped to avoid. However, finally in *Henry IV Part I*, I found my man. Hal was the hero I had been seeking. Now I could achieve – at least in my mind – feats of greatness. I hoped that – like him – I could be a Renaissance man, both academic and athletic. Like Hal, I did not

→

always see eye to eye with my father. Like Hal, I associated with a team full of Falstaffs, Poins and Bardolfs. In grotty taverns (which I yearned to frequent), underage laughs could be had.

I began to be convinced also that, like Hal, I would suddenly emerge from my cocoon and dramatically prove all my critics wrong.

However, now I am in the last days of my sixth year fast approaching the end of my secondary education. I have already filled out limp application forms for courses and jobs in which I struggled to list my heroic feats. My certainties have failed me. My transformation did not materialise as quickly as I wished – if indeed it ever will. I am not sure at all that I am like the heroic Hal.

Perhaps – it is just possible – that I will not make a remarkable emergence into adulthood. It is even possible in life that I am not the central character at all . . . or even a hero with a small 'h'. I may never become a secret agent despite the fact that my hair is now like Sean Connery's . . . was. Is it possible that in life I am only a minor player like one of the characters I always avoided looking at too closely? If so, perhaps it is just a matter of finding the right play – the play which was written for me – me, the minor character aspiring to be Heroic.

Commentary

Like Twain, this student is trying to reflect on early childhood. Also like Twain, he writes in a casual, colloquial style, with a gently humorous tone, poking fun at himself in his early days. He achieves his humour in fairly simple ways – by exaggeration, by laughing at himself, by using punctuation such as brackets and dashes to add little asides. There are plenty of examples of this style. After making himself sound ancient – 'as far back as I can remember' – he adds in brackets that he is only eighteen at time of writing. He also brackets in the final line of the first paragraph the fact that, like Robin Hood, he may have redistributed the wealth from old to young only in his own mind. The play on words, instead of rich to poor, perhaps suggesting money moving from parent to child.

He also paints some comical pictures of himself – having his hair cut and playing parts at Halloween. He reaches a sort of high point in the statement, 'I was destined for Greatness'. Then reality and adolescence begins.

There are ideas in this essay conveyed through the humour. It seems to be about growing up and realising with increasing maturity that he is not the centre of the world and the hero of every play but, in fact, he may just be a minor character in life's pageant. In a fairly subtle way, we see him growing from a mischievous young first year student (like Puck), to fourth year with his laddish culture, like Hal, with his rugby friends visiting taverns and not always seeing eye to eye with his father.

This structural device works well, as does the repetition of the 'hair' motif throughout.

This is personal writing which does contain reflection. The student is not simply narrating events of his childhood, but he is reflecting on his development from one stage to the next. It is the reflection that gives the essay value and makes it more applicable to the reader. We can all identify with the idea of growing up and maturing, although each of our 'stories' is unique.

The other strong aspect to this writing is the development and consistency in the tone. It is personal and we get a strong sense of the person who is speaking in a humorous way, poking fun as he gradually learns that all the planets do not revolve around him.

Task

Look again at your own piece of autobiography:

- Is there clear reflection on one or two ideas arising from the incidents related?
- Is there a structure which shows control – an effort to present material effectively?
- Does a persona or speaker emerge from the writing, probably through the adoption of a consistent tone? (It does not have to be humorous.)

Landscape/Nature writing: mood and structure

A writer may use a more complex structure than the strict chronology in an essay as an effective device for revealing the central concerns, the reflections. A more complex structure is evident in the following essay, which also has a mood or atmosphere and a strong element of 'nature'. This type of writing has acquired the label 'landscape essay'.

In *Darkness and Light*, Kathleen Jamie reflects on a winter journey made to the Orkneys. Three parts of this essay are presented here. In the opening of the piece she establishes the importance of darkness and light in her reflections; in the central section she reaches the dramatic moment or climax of her 'journey'; and in the conclusion, she returns to the different moods and reflections that she has established throughout her essay in each of these 'parts'.

A: Darkness and Light – *introduction*

Kathleen Jamie (2005)

Mid-December, the still point of the turning year. It was eight in the morning and Venus was hanging like a wrecker's light above the Black Craig. The hill itself – seen from our kitchen window – was still in silhouette, though the sky was lightening into a pale yellow-grey. It was a weakling light, stealing into the world like a thief through the window someone forgot to close.

The talk was all of Christmas shopping and kids' parties. Quietly, though, like a coded message, an invitation arrived to a meal to celebrate the winter solstice. Only six people would be there, and no electric light.

That afternoon – it was Saturday – we took the kids to the pantomime. This year it was *The Snow Queen*. She was oddly glittery, and swirled around the stage in a platinum cloak with her comic entourage of ravens and spiders. The heroes were a boy and a brave, north-travelling girl. At one point the Snow Queen, in her silver sledge, stormed off stage left, and had she kept going, putting a girdle round the earth, she'd have been following the 56th parallel. Up the Nethergate, out of Dundee across Scotland, away over the North Atlantic, she'd have made landfall over Labrador, swooped over Hudson's Bay, and have glittered like snowfall somewhere in southern Alaska. Crossing the Bering Sea, then the Sea of Okhotsk, she'd have streaked on through central Moscow, in time, if she really got a move on, to enter stage right for her next line. Of course, we have no realm of snow here, none of the complete Arctic darkness. Nonetheless, when it came time for the Snow Queen to be vanquished for another year, to melt down through a trap door leaving only her puddled cloak, everyone was cheered. Before she went, however, the ascendant Sun God kissed the Snow Queen in a quick, knowing, grown-up complicity. I liked that bit.

I like the precise gestures of the sun, at this time of year. When it eventually rises above the hill it shines directly into our small kitchen window. A beam crosses the table and illuminates the hall beyond. In barely an hour, though, the sun sinks again below the hill, south-southeast, leaving a couple of hours of dwindling half-light. Everything we imagine doing, this time of year, we imagine doing in the dark.

I imagined travelling into the dark. Northward – so it got darker as I went. I'd a notion to sail by night, to enter into the dark for the love of its textures and wild intimacy. I had been asking around among literary people, readers of books, for instances of dark as natural phenomenon, rather than as a cover for all that's wicked, but could find few. It seems to me that our cherished metaphor of darkness is wearing out.

→

Pity the dark: we're so concerned to overcome and banish it, it's crammed full of all that's devilish, like some grim cupboard under the stair. But dark is good. We are conceived and carried in the darkness, are we not? When my son was born, a midwinter child, he cried pitifully at the ward's lights, and only settled to sleep when he was laid in a big pram with a black hood under a black umbrella. Our vocabulary ebbs with the daylight, closes down with the cones of our retinas. I mean, I looked up 'darkness' on the Web – and was offered Christian ministries offering to lead me to salvation. And there is always death. We say death is darkness; and darkness death.

Initial thoughts

This opening is rich in ideas: it has a number of strands which you, as a reader, want to pick up at the beginning of the essay and follow to the conclusion to show careful reading and understanding. Read the passage again carefully and mark up some of the important ideas that occur to you as you read. You may wish then to compare your notes to the ones suggested below.

Paragraphs 1/2
- mid-December – 21st December – the Solstice – the turning point – shortest day of the year
- sets the scene with Venus, Black Craig in silhouette
- early morning light at home – kitchen; describing light as weak, pale, likening it to a thief – stealing through an open window
- a happy domestic scene – preparing for Christmas, shopping
- interesting invitation arrives 'quietly' to party for the solstice, only six people, no electric light

Paragraph 3
- it's Saturday and event is pantomime with kids – The Snow Queen
- words of cold – glittering and platinum; negative words of ravens and spiders
- writer imagines Snow Queen storming off stage in silver sledge, her travels around the world on 56th parallel to colder places than Dundee
- connects places like Labrador, Hudson's Bay, Alaska, Bering Sea, Okhotsk, Moscow and back in time for her next line
- this image gives a global perspective at northern latitudes to idea of darkness and cold

Paragraph 4
- writer returns to light coming in kitchen window – its precision – a beam across the table and into the hall
- brevity of time that it is visible and dwindling half light at this time of year – sun sinks in barely an hour
- everything we do at this time of year we do in darkness

Paragraph 5
- she imagines travelling into the dark – north – and it gets darker and darker; sailing by night
- mentions textures and intimacies which would make sense of touch more important in the dark – a good reflection at this point of passage

Paragraph 6
- writer reflects on darkness as metaphor – it seems always to represent evil, devilish things
- likens it to grim cupboard under the stairs (another domestic image), death
- then she establishes a case for what is good about darkness – we are born in darkness but concludes: 'We say death is darkness; and darkness death.' – another strong reflection

Jamie continues in her essay to tell about boarding the ferry at Aberdeen, bound for the Orkneys. Because this is a night sailing, she hopes to experience absolute darkness somewhere at sea. She is disappointed in this effort because, even alone on the deck, the lights and the music spoil the mood. Ironically, Elton John is singing, 'don't let the sun go down on me.'

In a later part of this essay, Jamie reaches Orkney where she wishes to see the mid-winter light in Maes Howe, a neolithic chambered cairn, a 5000-year-old tomb. In the following extract from the same essay, *Darkness and Light*, Jamie writes about the dramatic moment when she hopes to see the late afternoon light send a shaft across the cairn, as the early tomb builders had planned.

B: Darkness and Light – *climax*

You enter into the inner chamber of the tomb by a low passageway more than 25 feet long. It's more of a journey than a gateway. You don't have to crawl on hands and knees, but neither can you walk upright. The stone roof bears down on your spine; a single enormous slab of stone forms the wall you brush with your left shoulder. You must walk in that stooped position just a moment too long, so when you're admitted to the cairn two sensations come at once; you're glad to stand, and the other is a sudden appreciation of stone. You are admitted into a solemn place which is not a heart at all, or even a womb, but a cranium.

You are standing in a high, dim stone vault. There is a thick soundlessness like a recording studio, or a strongroom. A moment ago, you were in the middle of a field, with the wind and curlews calling. That world has been taken away, and the world you have entered into is not like a cave, but a place of artifice, of skill. Yes, that's it, what you notice when you stand and look around is cool, dry, applied skill. Across five thousand years you can still feel their self-assurance.

The walls are of red sandstone, dressed into long rectangles, with a tall sentry-like buttress in each corner to support the corralled roof. The passage to the outside world is at the base of one wall. Set waist-high into the other three are square openings into cells which disappear into the thickness of the walls. That's where they laid the dead, once the bones had been cleaned of flesh by weather and birds. The stone blocks which would once have sealed these graves lie on the gravel floor. And the point is, the ancients who built this tomb orientated it precisely: the long passageway faces exactly the setting midwinter sun. Consequently, for the few days around the winter solstice a beam of the setting sun shines along the passage, and onto the tomb's back wall. In recent years, people have crept along the passageway at midwinter to witness this, the complicit kiss. Some, apparently, find it overwhelming.

We crossed the field. The heron took to the air. I dawdled behind. My guide, the young Rob, was waiting at the entrance, which is just a low square opening at the bottom of the mound. I glanced back at the outside world, the road, the clouded sky over Hoy's hills, which did not look promising; then we crept inside and for a long minute walked doubled over, until Rob stood and I followed.

Inside was bright as a tube train, and the effect was brutal. I'd expected not utter darkness, but perhaps a wombish-red. Rob was carrying a torch but this light revealed every crack, every join and fissure in the ancient stonework. At once a man's voice said, 'Sorry, I'll switch it off,' but the moment was lost and, anyway, I'd been forewarned. As he sold me the ticket, Alan had told me that surveyors were inside the cairn, with all their equipment. 'A bit of a problem', was how he'd put it. And here they were. We entered the tomb and, in that fierce white light, it was like that moment which can occur in midlife, when you look at your mother and realise with a shock that she is old.

Initial thoughts

Paragraph 1
- 'You' makes the reader a participant in the experience
- more of a journey than a gateway – suggests that this is a life-changing situation
- describes approach to cairn and likens centre – not to heart or womb – but to the cranium

Paragraphs 2/3
- description of the stone vault – soundless and strong
- contrast to the outer position where curlews were calling
- outside world is gone: it is like a museum not a cave – 'a place of skill' over five thousand years old; red sandstone walls – 'dressed' stone rectangles
- crafted cells for placing the dead
- tomb oriented with skill and precision for setting midwinter sun to send rays into passage to witness the 'kiss' of the sun on the wall is an overwhelming experience

Paragraphs 4/5
- she enters tomb in expectation after walk across fields and long crawl down passageway
- 'a bit of a problem' is an understatement – the magic of the tomb at the solstice is lost
- shock of moment makes this scene a startling climax which writer has effectively created
- shock inside – 'bright as a tube train'
- uses the word 'brutal' – a very harsh word – for the light in the tomb
- light showed every crack and fissure
- also uses harsh word 'fierce' to describe light – sounds like it could kill or wound in battle
- workmen offer to turn light off, but it is too late – magic that connects past with present is lost
- likens moment of shock to a time when you suddenly realise that your mother is old

Analysis

Jamie reaches a high point or creates a climax at this point in the passage with the idea that the light at the solstice should be striking across the tomb. She has prepared us for this moment of the long journey: first with the light in her kitchen window in Dundee striking a particular point at this time of year, but also with the disappointment of her failure to find absolute darkness on the ferry to Orkney.

Even the failure to see the light the way she wished, however, provides her with further reflections upon her theme of darkness and light. The climax of this passage seems to have been achieved through Jamie giving us a shocking account of a reversal of what she had been expecting.

In the final part of *Darkness and Light*, Jamie retraces her steps to conclude her reflections. Make notes on the ways in which she picks up the threads of her thinking which she had established at the beginning of this essay. This helps to make this an effective conclusion to this piece, bringing it 'full circle', as well as contrasting the moods which she established initially.

C: Darkness and Light – *conclusion*

In Stromness' narrow, eighteenth-century street, it was time for coffee and cake and some Christmas shopping. I wandered into a toy shop, all bright and lit for Christmas, and in there picked up a silver plastic tiara. My little daughter had liked the Snow Queen; she would love this. Standing there in the bright shop with this ridiculous tiara in my hand, turning it so it sparkled, I was thinking about light. I suppose I'd been hoping for a trick of the light of Maes Howe. No, trick was the wrong word. The tomb-gilders had constructed their cairn to admit a single beam of solstice light: it was the bending of a natural phenomenon to a human end, somewhere between technology and art. But not art either: drama. 'Nowhere', said George Mackay Brown, 'is the drama of dark and light played out more starkly than in the north.' A very ancient drama, going right back to the Neolithic. Were they the first people, I wondered, to articulate this metaphor of light and dark, of life and death …

Then the shop-keeper said 'enjoy it while it lasts.'

'I'm sorry?'

She nodded toward the plastic tiara in my hand.

'My little girl used to love these things, all glittery and bright. But she's fourteen now, and wears nothing but black.' …

My ventures into light and dark had been ill-starred. I'd had no dramatic dark, neither at sea nor in the tomb, and no resurrecting beam of sunlight. But lasers are light, aren't they? Intensified, organised light. I'd crept into Maes Howe at solstice, hoping for Neolithic technology; what I'd found was the technology of the 21st century. Here were skilled people passing light over these same stones, still making measurements by light and time. That thought pleased me.

I don't know if the 25 or so people who crept into Maes Howe for the solstice were rewarded with a beam of light. And if it came, did they part to let it through, like a doctor at an accident? I was at home again by then, and we were going out for dinner.

The hallway of our friends' cottage was inviting in candlelight, as was the room, and the table. The curtains were open to show black night pressed against the windows. We were a merry company and in the warm candlelight we enjoyed a half-joking, symbolic meal. We ate stuffed red peppers, to symbolise, our host said, the rising sun. Sautéed carrot sticks were its warming rays, and green beans, presented with a flourish represented the shoots of spring. We cheered the beans, and drank a toast, because tonight was mid-winter's night, the night of the complicit kiss, and tomorrow the light would begin its return.

Initial thoughts

Paragraph 1

The writer has returned to the light and business of Stromness:

- 'all bright and lit for Christmas'
- remembering her daughter and the Snow Queen, she purchases a tiara which 'sparkles'
- she reminds us that she is still thinking about light
- she reflects on 'trick' of light which was supposed to occur at Maes Howe,
- realising that 'trick' is wrong word because ancient people built precisely with solstice in mind
- uses phrase 'bending of a natural phenomenon to a human end' – strong theme in essay

- thinks it is not really technology or art, but drama
- uses quote by George Mackay Brown – 'Nowhere is the drama of dark and light played out more starkly than in the north.'
- returns to reflection on metaphor – light and dark, life and death
- uses word 'black' as a finale to conversation in shop – colour of clothing

Paragraph 2

- reflects that her mission had been 'ill-starred' (referring to universe) because she did not get complete darkness at sea nor in tomb
- natural beam of sunlight had been outshone by 21st–century laser
- she takes some satisfaction in idea that, like Neolithic men, we are still using technology to pass light over same stones – measurements of light and time
- reaches conclusion she is satisfied with 'That thought pleased me.'

Paragraphs 3/4

- Jamie returns to beginning of the essay in concluding remarks, reminding us of dinner to celebrate solstice by candlelight
- reminds us also of the ancient custom of celebrating mid-winter's night – 'complicit kiss' because the next day brings the natural phenomenon of gradual lengthening of day's light

Analysis

This non-fiction essay is as carefully crafted as the ancient tomb which the author visits. Like her progress to and into the cairn, this essay is more of a 'journey' than a 'gateway'. She presents it as a life-changing event; or, at least, an event which has given her a great deal to reflect upon.

Although the essay has been abridged here, in its entirety it gives a complete reflection on the concept and reality of darkness and light and what this has meant to mankind from the very beginnings of times. Parallels are drawn between Neolithic and 21st-century technology in an effort to show the importance of and the precision employed in man's effort to capture significant light. This reflection runs throughout the passage, giving not only a timeless but also a global perspective to the concept of the mid-winter solstice.

The framework structure of the passage can add much to the reader's appreciation. The structure is like a Russian doll: one doll after another opens with establishing mood and offering reflection.

- It begins in a Dundee kitchen with an invitation to a dinner to celebrate the solstice and an observation of the light across the kitchen table at this time of year.
- It continues with the light and glitter of the festive seasonal Snow Queen pantomime and the idea of circling the globe at the 56th parallel, connecting all the places that share the same time element.
- The ferry journey to Orkney and the walk and entry to the cairn are part of the experience.
- Then the smallest 'doll' is the climax of the essay: the entry to the inner cairn in hopes of experiencing sunlight at the solstice and instead facing the glare of modern technology.

She closes 'the dolls' – the essay's reflections and moods – in the reverse order:

- She exits from the cairn, reflecting upon the timeless parallels between ancient man and modern times.
- She experiences the lights and gaiety of a Stromness street at Christmas time, buying a tiara for her daughter in memory of the Snow Queen.
- She returns to her Dundee home in time for the candlelit solstice dinner to recognise and celebrate again what mankind has celebrated since the beginnings of time.

The essay is effective in so many ways: structure, persona, tone, moods and imagery. It is important to recognise, particularly, how reflection on a landscape runs throughout this essay on a place.

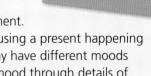

Task

You may wish first to write a reflective essay on a place or a landscape which is important to you or on an experience in which the location was a significant element.
Think carefully about the structure you use, perhaps a framework or a flashback using a present happening that causes you to reflect upon the past. Present moments and past moments may have different moods which makes your writing more interesting for the reader. Work on establishing mood through details of word choice and imagery.

Thinking about structure in such a way may help you to avoid the danger of pure narrative. Reflection is essential in your essay. The way you structure your essay, establishing mood in each section, may help the reader appreciate your experience and your ideas more fully.

Critical analysis of prose non-fiction: a summary

There is a systematic way of approaching non-fiction passages, although you may find your own approach. This is a suggestion:

1 Give some thought to the genre or type of non-fiction writing which is under consideration. It is not necessary to label it as biography/autobiography, memoir, landscape or nature writing, travel writing, book/television/film review ... but it may be helpful to think about the type. The easiest way to think about this is through the question format with which you are familiar:
- Who is the writer?
- Where is this taking place?
- What is happening?
- Why is the author writing (do you think)?
- When – or under what circumstances – is this taking place?
2 Try to bring as much clarity as you can to your understanding of the situation.
3 Is there an obvious structure to the passage or essay?
- Is it chronological? Sequential?
- Is there a flashback?
- Is there a circular structure? A series of stages building to a climax and the reverse order coming out of the essay or reaching a conclusion?
- Identify the climax or high point in the series of events – if there is one.
- Or, conversely, is there an anti-climax?
- Is there a series of arguments?
- What marks the changes or steps in the structure? Changes of mood, or scene, or tone?
- Are there signs of linkage between steps or stages?

4   How much can you tell about the persona or narrator or writer of the essay?
  - Is he or she a central figure or peripheral?
  - What is the relationship to the reader?
  - What tone is the persona/speaker/writer adopting?
5   How would you describe the writer's style (in detail)?
  - Is it descriptive?
  - Are images characteristic of the style or is it terse or matter-of-fact?
  - What effects are achieved?
  - Is the imagery consistent? Extended? Appropriate?
  - Are there particular words, phrases, images or styles that appeal/don't appeal to you?

This approach should give you a good start in writing an effective analysis and appreciation/evaluation of any non-fiction passage.

> **Note:** These pointers can also be a helpful approach to take when analysing critically your own creative writing.

DRAMA

Introduction

The following scenes from drama – some complete, some extracts – provide opportunities for the study of specific dramatic techniques and develop some of the skills you need to approach the analysis of drama. Each of the scenes concentrates on a specific technique but, of course, all of them can be used to demonstrate the use of other aspects. For example, an extract in which you are asked to focus on character, may also provide you with good examples of the use of conflict, climax, or any of the other techniques which will be dealt with in this section.

The basic approach which works for all these scenes is (as in the other sections) reading with concentration and noting or 'marking up' what seem to you to be the important areas/sentences/phrases/words even, which help you to gain an accurate understanding, deeper appreciation and evaluation of the techniques the dramatist uses.

Through practice and trial and error you will find a method of 'marking up' which suits you. It may be the use of highlighters, or underlining, or writing notes in the margin: what matters is that having a pen (or pencil) in your hand keeps your mind focused on the task in hand and makes your reading active, rather than passive.

After we have looked at the first exercise in this section (from *The Glass Menagerie*), you will see an example of one method of starting the 'marking-up' task for the opening 22 lines.

Characterisation

A

The Glass Menagerie

In this scene from *The Glass Menagerie* by Tennessee Williams (1945), Jim, a colleague of Tom's at the shoe warehouse where they both work, is arriving with Tom for supper at Tom's family's apartment.

> *(Tom gives a long ring)*
>
> Amanda: Preposterous goings on! Can you give me one reason – *(calls out lyrically)* Coming! Just one second! – why should you be afraid to open a door? Now you answer it Laura!
>
> 5   Laura: Oh, oh, oh … *(She returns to the other room, darts to the victrola* and winds it up frantically and turns it on)*
>
> Amanda: Laura Wingfield, you march right to that door!
>
> Laura: Yes – yes, Mother!
>
> *(A faraway, scratching rendition of Dardanella softens the air and gives her strength to move to the door. She draws it cautiously open. Tom enters with the caller, Jim O'Connor)*
>
> Tom: Laura, this is Jim. Jim, this is my sister Laura.

→

	Jim:	I didn't know that Shakespeare had a sister!
10	Laura:	*(retreating stiff and trembling from the door)* How – how do you do?
	Jim:	*(heartily extending his hand)* Okay!
		(Laura touches it hesitantly with hers.)
	Jim:	Your hand's cold, Laura!
	Laura:	Yes, well – I've been playing the victrola …
15	Jim:	Must have been playing classical music on it! You ought to play a little hot swing music to warm you up!
	Laura:	Excuse me – I haven't finished playing the victrola….
		(She turns awkwardly and hurries into the front room)
	Jim:	*(grinning)* What was the matter?
	Tom:	Oh – with Laura? Laura is – terribly shy.
20	Jim:	Shy, huh! It's unusual to meet a shy girl nowadays. I don't believe you ever mentioned you had a sister.
	Tom:	Well, now you know. I have one. Here is the Post Dispatch. You want a piece of it?
	Jim:	Uh-huh.
	Tom:	What piece? The comics?
25	Jim:	Sports! *(Glances at it)* Ole Dizzy Dean is on his bad behavior again.
	Tom:	*(disinterested)* Yeah? *(lights cigarette and crosses to the fire escape door)*
	Jim:	Where are you going?
	Tom:	I'm going out on the terrace.
30	Jim:	*(goes after him)* You know, Shakespeare – I'm going to sell you a bill of goods!
	Tom:	What goods?
	Jim:	A course I'm taking.
	Tom:	Huh?
	Jim:	In public speaking! You and me, we're not the warehouse type.
35	Tom:	Thanks – that's good news. But what has public speaking got to do with it?
	Jim:	It fits you for – executive positions!
	Tom:	Awww.
	Jim:	I tell you it's done a helluva lot for me.
	Tom:	In what respect?
40	Jim:	In every! Ask yourself what is the difference between you an' me and the men in the office down front? Brains? – No! – Ability? – No! Then what? Just one little thing –
	Tom:	What is that one little thing?

45	Jim:	Primarily it amounts to – social poise! Being able to square up to people and hold your own on any social level!
	Amanda:	*(off stage)* Tom?
	Tom:	Yes, mother?
	Amanda:	Is that you and Mr O'Connor?
	Tom:	Yes, Mother.
50	Amanda:	Ask Mr O'Connor if he would like to wash his hands.
	Jim:	Aw, no – no – thank you – I took care of that at the warehouse. Tom –
	Tom:	Yes?
	Jim:	Mr Mendoza was speaking to me about you.
	Tom:	Favourably?
55	Jim:	What do you think?
	Tom:	Well –
	Jim:	You're going to be out of a job if you don't wake up.
	Tom:	I am waking up –
	Jim:	You show no signs.
60	Tom:	The signs are interior.
		I'm planning to change. *(speaking with quiet exhilaration)* I'm right on the point of committing myself to a future that doesn't include the warehouse, and Mr Mendoza or even a night-school course in public speaking.
65	Jim:	What are you gassing about?
	Tom:	I'm tired of the movies.
	Jim:	Movies!
	Tom:	Yes, movies! Look at them – *(he waves towards the marvels of Grand Avenue)* All of those glamorous people – having adventures – hogging it all, gobbling the whole thing up! You know what happens? People go to the movies instead of moving! Hollywood characters are supposed to have all the adventures for everybody in America, while everybody in America sits in a dark room and watches them have them! Yes, until there's a war. That's when adventure becomes available to the masses! Everyone's dish, not only Gable's!* The people in the dark room come out of the dark room to have some adventure themselves – Goody, goody – It's our turn now, to go to the South Sea Islands – to make a safari – to be exotic, far-off! – But I'm not patient. I don't want to wait till then. I'm tired of the movies and I am about to move!
80	Jim:	Move?
	Tom:	Yes.
	Jim:	When?

	Tom:	Soon!
	Jim:	Where? Where?
		(Tom searches in his pockets)
85	Tom:	I'm starting to boil inside. I know I seem dreamy, but inside – well, I'm boiling! – Whenever I pick up a shoe, I shudder a little thinking how short life is and what I'm doing! – Whatever that means, I know it doesn't mean shoes – except as something to wear on a traveller's feet! *(finds paper)* Look –
90	Jim:	What?
	Tom:	I'm a member.
	Jim:	*(reading)* The Union of Merchant Seamen.
	Tom:	I paid my dues this month, instead of the light bill.
	Jim:	You will regret it when they turn the lights off.
95	Tom:	I won't be here.
	Jim:	How about your mother?
	Tom:	I'm like my father. The bastard son of a bastard! *(looking at his photograph back in the room)* See how he grins? And he's been absent going on sixteen years!
100	Jim:	You're just talking, you drip. How does your mother feel about it?
	Tom:	Shhh! – Here comes Mother! Mother is not acquainted with my plans!

Tennessee Williams (1945)

*victrola – an early form of phonograph/record player.
*Clark Gable – a Hollywood film star mainly of the 1930s and 1940s.

Task

Think about how the character of Tom is presented in this scene. You should consider not only his dialogue but also his relationships with the other characters in the scene. Mark up the text accordingly.

There are basic questions you have to ask about the text to make sure that you understand what is going on in the scene – that you don't mistake, for example, who is who in a family, or what the setting is in time or place. The same process is explained in the section on fiction (pages 40–41, 48, 58–59, 61, 65).

* Who?
* Where?
* When?
* What?
* Why?
* How?

Initial thoughts

The main part of the scene is a conversation between Jim and Tom revealing their thoughts about their future.

Amanda (Tom's mother) appears to be quite a dominant/domineering character – she seems to force Laura to go to answer the door, although she is unwilling to do so. Laura herself appears to be scared to answer the door and uses her victrola as an exit strategy.

At the end of the scene Tom appears to be about to abandon the family, without telling his mother.

So we know **who** the characters are.

When and **where** – the date in the introduction (1945) and the mention of the war suggest that the play is contemporaneous with the date of its writing. It is set in a city in the United States. (It is, in fact, St Louis, but that is not particularly relevant.)

What happens is clearly set out.

Why? The answer to this question is sometimes not immediately apparent, until you have looked carefully into the scene – but it has to do with the central concerns. What are the important ideas?

How? This involves an analysis of the dramatic techniques used by the writer.

Analysis

The characters are presented in very obvious ways.

- Amanda is seen as almost bullying her daughter – 'Laura Wingfield, you march right to that door!' These are almost in military terms – the use of her surname and 'march' and 'right to'.
- Laura displays an abnormal shyness – her use of the victrola to divert her feelings of what appears to be panic; her handshake 'touches it tentatively with her own' – and when she does speak she says the absolute minimum and can't wait to escape.
- Jim is shown in this little greeting scene to be open and friendly – making easy conversation with Laura, trying to 'warm' her a little (metaphorically) by talking about music, 'a little hot swing music'.

Tom has obviously not mentioned Laura to Jim previously which perhaps suggests that he feels he has to conceal her (or her weakness) and that it bothers him – look at the change of subject in lines 21–22.

Jim and Tom represent two approaches to their futures. Jim is a 'striver' after the much talked about 'American Dream'. 'We're not the warehouse types'; Jim's nickname for Tom – Shakespeare – suggests that he has a respect for Tom's intellectual qualities.

His solution is to 'improve' himself by studying at night classes, while retaining his job at the warehouse.

He tries to encourage Tom to do likewise 'You know, Shakespeare, I'm going to sell you a bill of goods.'

Tom seems entirely unimpressed – his monosyllabic replies contrast with Jim's enthusiasm.

The **turning point** in the scene is when Jim mentions Mr Mendoza – their boss. 'You're going to be out of a job if you don't wake up' sparks off a reaction in Tom.

'Wake up' is the key phrase. It sets off in Tom an impassioned speech about his desire for adventure. He has realised that his habit of escapism – going to the movies to experience adventure – is at best a second-hand experience which is supposed to satisfy the populace in general, and at worst a failure of his own will to make any changes. His remark about the war allowing people to have adventures seems odd, but the US forces were at that time involved in the war in the Pacific, and travelling to 'exotic' places.

Note: the greater your general knowledge of history, politics, science, art etc., the more you can get into the detail of texts you are presented with.

Tom's **tone** here is disparaging of the whole movie thing. He uses a pun at the end of the speech – 'I'm tired of the movies and I am about to move'.

'I'm boiling' and his reference to 'shoes' – the ones he has to deal with in the warehouse being transformed into 'something to wear on a traveller's feet' – show his pent-up frustration with his job.

He produces his Seaman's Union card almost like a rabbit out of a hat – as proof to Jim, and maybe even to himself, that he does intend to go.

There is a **contrast** between Tom and Jim, the stable common-sense character who asks the obvious question – about his mother.

Tom knows he's behaving, or going to behave, badly: he calls himself a 'bastard son'.

'Shhh' (as his mother approaches) produces an anti-climax: he has obviously not had the courage to tell her yet.

The scene has the effect of winning some sympathy for Tom in his restlessness, and the oppressive atmosphere created by his mother, but less sympathy when we think of the fact that he is leaving Laura too, and is going about things in a rather cowardly way.

Actions and **dialogue** are giving us the information we need to understand the characters presented in this scene. Unlike fiction, there is no narrative voice to tell us more.

The central concerns – the answer to the 'Why?' question – seem to be related to the idea of conflict between personal freedom and family responsibilities, and the illusory nature of escapism in popular culture (movies).

Marking up

In reading, you are on the lookout for significant words/phrases/actions that help you to answer the basic questions – but you are also looking for ones which will help you to answer the particular question you have been asked.

Amanda: Preposterous goings on! Can you give me one reason – (calls out lyrically) Coming! Just one second! – why should you be afraid to open a door? Now you answer it Laura!

'lyrically' suggests an artificiality

suggests pathological panic

Laura: Oh, oh, oh … (She returns to the other room, darts to the victrola* and winds it up frantically and turns it on)

Amanda: Laura Wingfield, you march right to that door!

use of her surname and strong command words suggest military domination?

Laura: Yes – yes, Mother!

(A faraway, scratching rendition of Dardanella softens the air and gives her strength to move to the door. She draws it cautiously open.

this is surprising if they have been work colleagues. Why?

Tom enters with the caller, Jim O'Connor)

Tom: Laura, this is Jim. Jim, this is my sister Laura.

Jim: I didn't know that Shakespeare had a sister!

emphasises her fear

Laura: (retreating stiff and trembling from the door)

a pointer to Jim's open character

How – how do you do?

Jim: (heartily extending his hand) Okay!

(Laura touches it hesitantly with hers.)

she can just about cope

Jim: Your hand's cold, Laura!

Laura: Yes, well – I've been playing the victrola …

genial, friendly, trying humour

Jim: Must have been playing classical music on it! You ought to play a little hot swing music to warm you up!

Laura: Excuse me – I haven't finished playing the victrola…

a really lame exit line/excuse

(She turns awkwardly and hurries into the front room)

Jim: (grinning) What was the matter?

pause suggests perhaps more than ordinarily shy

Tom: Oh – with Laura? Laura is – terribly shy.

Jim: Shy, huh! It's unusual to meet a shy girl nowadays. I don't believe you ever mentioned you had a sister.

- short, declarative sentence shutting off further comment
- newspaper used as distraction/ change of subject

Tom: Well, now you know. I have one. Here is the Post Dispatch. You want a piece of it?

You may find it difficult to begin with to see what you should be noting, and often you will notice more on a second reading – once you know what you are looking for.

Among these it is likely that there will be:

- elements of characterisation in dialogue – often words suggesting emotional states or tone

- elements of characterisation suggested by stage directions

- sections/phrases that you do not understand on first reading – and they are likely to be important, so note them for further study

- structural points – pauses, changes of direction, climax

- imagery, symbolism.

These techniques will be explored in other extracts in this section, and will increase your ability to see more, and more quickly, as you read.

Note: Remember that although we are reading these extracts, their true place is on stage, and stage directions – which are mostly messages from the writer to the director/ actor – are important in helping us identify the emotions/motivation of the characters.

How you make your notes is entirely up to you. Colour has been used in the above example, but the use of different types of underlining, or circling, or notes in the margin, or highlighting, or any combination of these can be helpful.

B

School for Scandal

This is the opening scene from *School for Scandal* by Richard Brindsley Sheridan (1777).

Act One, Scene One

Lady Sneerwell's House.

Lady Sneerwell at the dressing table. Mr Snake drinking chocolate.

Lady S: The paragraphs, you say, Mr Snake, were all inserted?

Snake: They were, madam; and as I copied them myself in a feigned hand, there can be no suspicion whence they came.

Lady S: Did you circulate the report of Lady Brittle's intrigue with Captain Boastall?

5 Snake: That's in as fine a train as your ladyship could wish. In the common course of things, I think it must reach Mrs Clackit's ears within four-and-twenty hours; and then, you know, the business is as good as done.

Lady S: Why, truly, Mrs Clackit has a very pretty talent, and a great deal of industry.

Snake: True, madam, and has been tolerably successful in her day. To my knowledge
10 she has been the cause of six matches being broken off, and three sons disinherited; of four forced elopements, and as many close confinements; nine separate maintenances, and two divorces. Nay, I have more than once traced her causing a tête-à-tête in the Town and Country Magazine when the parties, perhaps, had never seen each other's face before in the course of their lives.

→

15	Lady S:	She certainly has talent, but her manner is gross.
	Snake:	'Tis very true, – She generally designs well. Has a free tongue and a bold invention; but her colouring is too dark, and her outlines often extravagant. She wants the delicacy of tint, and mellowness of sneer, which distinguish your ladyship's scandal.
20	Lady S:	You are partial, Snake.
	Snake:	Not in the least – everybody allows that Lady Sneerwell can do more with a word or look, than can many with the most labored detail, even when they happen to have a little truth on their side to support it.
25	Lady S:	Yes, my dear Snake; and I am no hypocrite to deny the satisfaction I reap from the success of my efforts. Wounded myself in the early part of my life, by the envenomed tongue of slander, I confess I have since known no pleasure equal to reducing others to the level of my own injured reputation.
30	Snake:	Nothing could be more natural. But, Lady Sneerwell, there is one affair in which you have lately employed me, wherein, I confess, I am at a loss to guess your motives.
	Lady S:	I conceive you mean with respect to my neighbour, Sir Peter Teazle, and his family.
35	Snake:	I do. Here are two young men, to whom Sir Peter has acted as a kind of guardian since their father's death; the eldest possessing the most amiable character, and universally well-spoken of; the youngest, the most dissipated and extravagant young fellow in the kingdom, without friends or character: the former an avowed admirer of your ladyship's, and apparently your favourite; the latter attached to Maria, Sir Peter's ward, confessedly beloved by her. Now, on the face of these circumstances, it is utterly unaccountable to me, why you, the widow of a city knight, with a good jointure, should not close with the passion of a man of such character and expectations as Mr Surface; and more so why you should be so uncommonly earnest to destroy the mutual attachment subsisting between his brother and Maria.
40		
45	Lady S:	Then at once to unravel this mystery, I must inform you, that love has no share whatever in the intercourse between Mr Surface and me.
	Snake:	No!
	Lady S:	His real attachment is to Maria, or her fortune; but finding his brother a favoured rival, he has been obliged to mask his pretensions, and profit by my assistance.
50	Snake:	Yet still I am more puzzled why you should interest yourself in his success.
	Lady S:	How dull you are! Cannot you surmise the weakness which I hitherto, through shame, have concealed even from you? Must I confess that Charles, that libertine, that extravagant, that bankrupt in fortune and reputation, that he it is for whom I am thus anxious and malicious, and to gain whom I would sacrifice everything?
55		
	Snake:	Now, indeed, your conduct appears consistent; but how came you and Mr Surface so confidential?

→

60	Lady S:	For our mutual interest. I have found him out a long time since. I know him to be artful, selfish and malicious – in short, a sentimental* knave; while with Sir Peter, and indeed with all his acquaintance, he passes for a miracle of prudence, good sense, and benevolence.
	Snake:	Yes; yet Sir Peter vows he has not his equal in England, and above all, he praises him as a man of sentiment*.
65	Lady S:	True – and with the assistance of his sentiment and his hypocrisy he has brought Sir Peter entirely into his interest with regard to Maria, while poor Charles has no friend in the house, though, I fear, he has a powerful one in Maria's heart, against whom we must direct our schemes.

Richard Brindsley Sheridan (1777)

* the eighteenth-century meaning of these words is concerned with the artificial or exaggerated show of feelings.

Think about what you learn about the two characters in this scene and their relationship with each other. Before you look at the explication of the text which follows, try to answer the first four basic questions: Who? Where? When? What?

Initial thoughts

Make sure that you use the information you are given as an introduction to the extract.

In this case you are dealing with an unfamiliar society, and a period in drama which you probably have not come across in your studies in English or Drama.

Start with the date 1777 and the title 'School for Scandal'.

Period before the French Revolution (1789) – period of aristocratic excess? King George III on the throne. Coffee houses. Gossip.

If you have studied history, you might think that you have an advantage, but some common knowledge of the French Revolution got from reading or film – for example, *A Tale of Two Cities*, or of the film/stage play *The Madness of King George* could help to suggest the social background of the time. (The wider your reading, and the greater the extent of your general knowledge, the more you can bring to a text.)

And the script itself talks about gossip or 'scandal'.

Who?

Lady Sneerwell: names obviously include a character sketch – so, she sneers, but does so with style (a lady).

Snake: presumably has the attributes of a snake – devious, slimy, poisonous...

Already you are aware that this is not a 'naturalistic' drama. That there are 'attitudes' and probably some humour – although it may be a satire, rather than a comedy.

Mrs Clackit: another gossip

Sir Peter Teazle: his two sons 'Mr Surface' (again an indication of character) and Charles (the younger son), and Maria (his ward).

When?

The date is given and you have no reason the believe that the events are not of that period – see information above.

Where?

Somewhere society people gather – London most probably.

What is happening?

Snake appears to be acting for Lady Sneerwell in spreading gossip:

* lines 1–3 – 'the paragraphs' in a 'feigned hand' (written gossip)
* lines 4–8 – and 'the report' through Mrs Clackit (verbal gossip)

Lady Sneerwell seems to like throwing spanners in the works and causing upset and injury.

The family of Sir Peter Teazle is a particular target for her deviousness.

Analysis

You have already looked at Lady S and Snake. Mrs Clackit (given the description inherent in her name) is also a vicious gossip – the exaggeration of lines 9–19 confirm the view that a satiric tone is being developed.

Snake's speech – lines 33–43 – is giving a great deal of information about the Teazle family – in a way which could be regarded as a bit unsubtle.

The elder son and Lady S appear to be potentially a pair; the younger son and Maria appear to be in love.

But Lady S is not finalising her relationship with the older brother and is trying to demolish the relationship of the younger brother.

The character of 'Mr Surface' (the older brother) is given partly by his name, and also by the report that he is after Maria because of her fortune.

The character of the younger brother, Charles, is painted as extravagant/bankrupt/a libertine.

Mr Surface's and Lady S's characters are furthered by the fact that we are told that each is as bad as the other, and that they have managed to convince Sir Peter, the guardian of Maria, that Mr Surface is good and Charles is bad.

The scene ends with Snake and Lady S starting to plot more falsehood to get Maria to renounce her love for Charles and transfer it to Mr Surface, so that Lady S can get Charles, and Mr Surface can get Maria's money.

There is a lot of exposition in this scene, but it is necessary to introduce character, plot and theme. The presentation of the characters seems a little two-dimensional to the modern reader/audience – but the audience was aware that the action was stylised, and that they were not meant to like these two people – although one could admire their skill in the propagation of 'Scandal' – which again shows the importance of the title.

Why? What appears to be the point? The damage that gossip can do – a satiric look at the society in which this happens?

How is characterisation built in this scene?

The dialogue between the characters; Lady Sneerwell's superior position; the motives suggested by the dialogue; their attitudes as suggested by their names.

Characterisation: creative writing

Having studied these scenes, with the focus on characterisation, the next task is for you to attempt writing a script for yourself.

Then you should apply the same skills of analysis to your own (or your fellow students') work by editing.

In these examples, the editing is done on the same principles, using the same colours, replacements, deletions, etc. as is demonstrated in the examples in the prose fiction section – pages 44–45, 53, 67.

Jim

A care home. An elderly resident and a carer. The carer sits down beside the old man in the lounge.

Carer: How are you today, Jim?

Jim: I'm fine thanks.

Carer: Would you like a cup of tea?

Jim: That would be lovely.

The carer brings tea from a nearby trolley and hands it to the old man.

5 Jim: Thank you, dear.

The carer sits down again.

Jim: I haven't seen my daughter for a long time.

Carer: Jim, she was in yesterday. We were speaking to her about her holiday, do you remember?

Pause.

Jim: Oh, was she? Are you sure?

10 Carer: Yes, she stayed until around about lunchtime.

Pause.

→

Jim: I don't think you're right. ~~Like I said,~~ I haven't seen my daughter for a long time.

Pause.

15 Jim: Is there any chance of a cup of tea this morning?

Carer: Jim, I made you one just minutes ago. Look, it's on the coffee table right beside you.

Jim: That's not mine, that's old Andy's!

20 Carer: Jim, that's ~~definitely~~ your tea.

Jim: ~~I don't take milk.~~ That can't be mine.

The carer rises from her seat, returning to the tea trolley to make another cup of tea.

Carer: There you go Jim, a nice cup of tea.

Jim: Wonderful. Thank you my dear.

Pause.

Jim: What day is it today?

25 Carer: It's Thursday today.

Jim: Oh. Thanks.

~~As the conversation between the carer and the old man continues, Jim starts to become very confused.~~

Jim: Dear, can I ask you something?

Carer: ~~What's up?~~ Of course.

Jim: What day is it today?

30 Carer: ~~It's Thursday, like I said earlier.~~ It's Thursday.

Jim: ~~That's the first time I've asked.~~ (slowly) Have I asked that before?

~~Carer: If you say so.~~

Pause. Jim looks lost.

Carer: (realising his confusion) Of course not. Would you like a game of dominoes before lunch?

35 Jim: No thanks, dear. I'd rather have forty winks.

Pause.

Jim: Do you think my daughter will visit me soon?

Commentary

Someone of Jim's age would not say 'like I said'.

Remove 'definitely' – it is too negative on the carer's part.

Jim's original reply is not convincing. The carer would know about milk or no milk.

The use of stage directions here is wrong. The dialogue must show the confusion. **Stage directions should not be used to shortcut the process.**

'What's up?' does not fit with the carer's tone.

Lines 28 and 30 are too sharp and uncaring. The replacements elicit more understanding and sympathy for both Jim and the carer.

For all drama writing check, by speaking the text out loud, that the dialogue sounds natural and credible.

Old friends

A busy high street. A woman is walking whilst rummaging in her bag. Turns into the doorway of a coffee shop. Another woman is coming out of said coffee shop. They bump shoulders.

	Helen:	Sorry
	Claire:	Helen Baxter?
	Helen:	Claire?
	Claire:	Oh my God, Helen! How are you?
5	Helen:	Fine thanks–
	Claire:	You look amazing!
	Helen:	Thanks, you're looking great as–
	Claire:	Well isn't it a small world?
	Helen:	That's what they tell–
10	Claire:	Do you know I don't think I've seen you since ooh … final fling it must have been.
	Helen *(bitterly)*:	That's right. You got off with James right in front of me, then you threw up in Mrs Arton's Fiorelli*.
15	Claire *(laughs)*:	Oh yes … oh, awfully sorry … I'd forgotten … did em … did people see that?
	Helen:	'Fraid so.
		Pause
		That old bat deserved what came to her bag, anyway. Remember that time we caught her trying to light a fag with a Bunsen burner?
20	Claire *(laughing)*:	And that time she locked us all in over lunch because she thought someone had put ethanol in her tea?
	Helen:	Mad old cow.
	Claire:	Poor dear.
	Helen:	Bitch.
		Pause
	Claire:	Yes … she didn't seem quite all there.
25	Helen:	On the sauce, probably.
	Claire:	Probably dead by now, poor thing.
	Helen:	Good riddance.
	Claire:	Yes … no family either … such a shame really …
		Pause
		Anyway, what are YOU up to now?
30	Helen:	I'm a–

→

Claire:	Last I heard you were studying for your final exams! Seems such a long time ago now–
Helen:	Yeah, I'm a lawyer now. For an insurance company.
Claire:	Oh … how lovely!! That must be terribly exciting!

Pause

35   *Widow! Yes that's right, husband died in the Falklands I think. Never was the same since, apparently. My mum was at school with her. Right character she used to be, by all accounts.*

Helen:	Who?
Claire:	Julia Arton of course!
40 Helen:	Oh right, of course.

Pause

So what do you do now?

Claire:	Full-time mum, that's me! Oh but they keep me busy, always on my feet, always ferrying them around. But they're ever so funny! My youngest, Ella – just turned two she has – we're potty training her at the moment, she's terribly funny – blows a raspberry every time she needs the toilet–
Helen:	Wonderful.
Claire:	Hang on, I've a video somewhere … where's my phone got to? … wait 'til you see it, she's so cute..
Helen:	That's alright; I'm actually meeting someone now, better get going y'know.
Claire:	Oh yes, me too! Busy, busy, busy! I've to pick up Jimmy Junior from karate now. Anyway, lovely to have seen you! I must tell Sandra I bumped into you.
Helen:	Alright, you too, bye now.
55 Claire:	Alright bye! See you later! Bye, bye, bye.

*Fiorelli – designer handbag.

Commentary

There are two separate little dramas going on here. Each is in its own way quite competent. The beginning and the end show Claire as the dominant, egocentric one of the pair – Helen hardly gets a word in edgeways: almost everything we know is about Claire, and Helen's desire to get away before the photos on the phone are found is entirely understandable. The only weakness in the dialogue is in the last two lines – there might be a more imaginative way of rounding the scene off.

The highlighted sections are all about their memories of Julia Arton, one of their teachers. In these sections, Claire is the kind, compassionate, forgiving one, whereas Helen is seen as hard and careless. Again it is quite well done – Claire's train of thought develops quite 'naturally' through this section despite Helen's interjections, and attempts to move on to other subjects.

Some work needs to be done to merge these two 'sketches', or each could be developed separately.

For all drama writing check, by speaking the text out loud, that the dialogue is natural and credible.

Structure

Dunsinane

In *Dunsinane* by David Greig (2010), Malcolm, the presumed heir to the throne of Scotland, has defeated Macbeth in a battle at Dunsinane with the help of an English army under Siward. Macbeth's wife, who had a powerful political position in her own right, has been reported as having committed suicide before the battle.

The Great Hall in Dunsinane.

Malcolm is on the throne.

	Siward:	You told me she was dead.
	Malcolm:	Did I?
	Siward:	You told me she went mad and died.
	Malcolm:	Mmm.
5	Siward:	You told me the tyrant had lost the support of the chiefs and he had no son and his queen had died of madness and so there would be no resistance to you but on the other hand we were likely to see a swift and general acceptance of your rule and the chance to establish a new and peaceful order.
10		That's what you said.
	Malcolm:	Yes.
	Siward:	Well – she's not dead.
	Malcolm:	So it would seem.
	Siward:	Not even sick.
15	Malcolm:	No.
	Siward:	You lied to me.
	Malcolm:	Siward – there's a small thing I ought to say if you don't mind – and I'm not trying to avoid your general point, but there's an important clarification I must make before we go any further. In Scotland to call me
20		a liar is really unacceptable – if – here in the great hall for example – a man were to call me a liar that would – essentially – demand a violent response being – as it would be – a matter of honour – and so usually the way we manage this sort of thing in Scotland is by being very careful not only not to tell lies – but also to be very very careful about the way we
25		hear and understand words. So for example – if a person in Scotland says 'It seems a person has died' we tend to hear that word 'seems' – and of course that word makes a difference. Isn't that infuriating? It's silly and of course it means that every discussion is fraught and people have to pussyfoot around when obviously one simply wants to cut through the
30		nonsense and describe the facts of the world as they are – but there it is – that's how things are – and so – before we go any further – I suppose what I'm asking you – Siward is – really – and this is just for clarification – are you calling me a liar?

→

	Siward:	No.
35	Malcolm:	Well, that's a relief.
	Siward:	I understood that the Queen was dead.
	Malcolm:	It turns out that that was a mistaken understanding.
	Siward:	It would seem so.
	Malcolm:	Mmm.

Pause

40		Of course the whole thing would be easier if she were dead.
	Siward:	What?
	Malcolm:	Well, as long as she's alive she will tend to be a focus for dissent.
	Siward:	I thought you said the chiefs were simply waiting for you to arrive and establish yourself before they would pledge their allegiance and crown
45		you king.
	Malcolm:	Siward, – do you mind if I ask – are you going to continue with this insistent literalness? 'You said' – 'He said' – you sound like a child.
	Siward:	I'm sorry.
		It seems I was mistaken in my understanding about the Queen.
50		I was also – apparently – mistaken in my understanding about dissent.
		Is there anything else in Scotland about which my understanding may have been mistaken.
	Malcolm:	I know. I know. It's quite ridiculous isn't it? I'm King of this country and even I don't understand it.
55		Sometimes I think you could be born in this country. Live in it all your life. Study it. Travel the length and breadth of it. And still – if someone asked you – to describe it – all you would be able to say without fear of contradiction is – 'It's cold.'
	Siward:	Is there anything else about the current situation in Scotland about
60		which my understanding may have been mistaken?
	Malcolm:	One thing.
	Siward:	What?
	Malcolm:	She has a son.

Task

Think about how the structure of this scene clarifies the bases of contention between Malcolm and Siward. Mark up the text showing how the scene is divided into three parts, each of which deals with a conflict of opinion.

This little scene is almost complete in itself, in that it deals with one set of circumstances, two characters, and has a beginning, a middle and an end.

There appears to be a conflict between Malcolm and Siward. Siward seems to feel that he has been misled by Malcolm, and is aggrieved by this.

Malcolm appears to be putting Siward in his place – or trying to placate him.

Analysis

Structure

In Siward's speech (lines 5–10) he states three things which he had been assured of:

- 'the tyrant had lost the support of the chiefs'
- 'he had no son'
- 'his queen had died of madness'

Each of these three is then demolished:

- The Queen's death – lines 1–38
- The chiefs' support – lines 39–52
- There is a son – lines 59–63

The final revelation, about the son, is the most important and makes the climax of this little scene, leaving Siward, one supposes, in a state of disbelief/rage/frustration. It is theatrically effective.

Tone

What is the tone of Malcolm's long speech (lines 17–33)?

Warning or conciliatory, or both?

You should try to pick out the words/phrases which have a conciliatory tone.

There are many – a few being:

- 'if you don't mind'
- 'I'm not trying to avoid your general point' (but he actually is avoiding it)
- 'Isn't that infuriating?'
- 'really – and this is just for clarification …'

And the warning tone:

- 'really unacceptable'
- 'demand a violent response'
- 'by being very, very careful'
- 'really – and this is just for clarification – are you calling me a liar?'

The tone is also promoted by the number of little pauses throughout, which have the effect of suggesting a measured and entirely reasonable discourse with an entirely reasonable man.

→

Siward tries to calibrate his tone in his answers to the explanation/warning he has just been given.

- 'I <u>understood</u> that the Queen was dead.'
- 'It would <u>seem</u> so.'

This little game is played out twice more.

Siward persists with his last question, and the answer is, of course, from his point of view the most serious of the three.

As a summing up of character, Malcolm is presented as devious and cunning; Siward as straightforward and unsubtle, but by no means stupid.

The **climax** of the scene – 'She has a son.' – is theatrically effective and seems likely to be the starting point for a new and important strand in the play.

Theatrical form: absurd drama

Last to Go

This is a complete revue sketch by Harold Pinter (1961).

A coffee stall. A Barman and an old Newspaper Seller. The Barman leans on his counter, the Old Man stands with tea.

	Man:	You was a bit busier earlier.
	Barman:	Ah.
	Man:	Round about ten.
	Barman:	Ten, was it?
5	Man:	About then.
		Pause
		I passed by here about then.
	Barman:	Oh yes?
	Man:	I noticed you were doing a bit of trade.
		Pause
10	Barman:	Yes, trade was very brisk here about ten.
	Man:	Yes, I noticed.
		Pause
		I sold my last one about then. Yes. About nine forty-five.
15	Barman:	Sold your last then, did you?

	Man:	Yes, my last 'Evening News' it was. Went about twenty to ten.	
		Pause	
		Sometimes it's the 'Star' is the last to go.	20
	Barman:	Ah.	
	Man:	Or the … whatshisname.	
	Barman:	'Standard'.	25
	Man:	Yes.	
		Pause	
		All I had left tonight was the 'Evening News'	
		Pause	
	Barman:	Then that went, did it?	
	Man:	Yes	30
		Pause	
		Like a shot.	
		Pause	

Barman:	You didn't have any left, eh?	
Man:	No. Not after I sold that one.	
	Pause	
35 Barman:	It was after that you must have come by here then, was it?	
Man:	Yes, I come by here after that, see, after I packed up.	
40 Barman:	You didn't stop here though, did you?	
Man:	When?	
Barman:	I mean, you didn't stop here and have a cup of tea then, did you?	
45 Man:	What, about ten?	
Barman:	Yes.	
Man:	No, I went up to Victoria.	
Barman:	No, I thought I didn't see you.	
Man:	I had to go up to Victoria.	
	Pause	
50 Barman:	Yes, trade was very brisk here about then.	
	Pause	
Man:	I went to see if I could get hold of George.	
Barman:	Who?	
55 Man:	George.	
	Pause	
Barman:	George who?	
Man:	George … whatshisname.	
Barman:	Oh.	
	Pause	
	Did you get hold of him?	
60 Man:	No. No, I couldn't get hold of him. I couldn't locate him.	
Barman:	He's not about much now, is he?	
	Pause	

Man:	When did you last see him then?	65
Barman:	Oh, I haven't seen him for years.	
Man:	No, nor me.	
	Pause	
Barman:	Used to suffer very bad from arthritis.	70
Man:	Arthritis?	
Barman:	Yes.	
Man:	He never suffered from arthritis.	
Barman:	Suffered very bad.	75
	Pause	
Man:	Not when I knew him.	
	Pause	
Barman:	I think he must have left the area.	
	Pause	
Man:	Yes, it was the 'Evening News' was the last to go tonight.	80
Barman:	Not always the last though, is it, though?	
Man:	No. Oh no. I mean sometimes it's the 'News'. Other times it's one of the others. No way of telling beforehand. Until you've got your last one left, of course. Then you can tell which one it's going to be.	85 / 90
Barman:	Yes.	
	Pause	
Man:	Oh yes.	95
	Pause	
	I think he must have left the area.	

This sketch has the advantage of being a complete little drama in a short space, which allows us to look at character and structure and central concerns and theatrical technique all in the same text.

Initial thoughts

Your first thoughts are probably 'What's this all about?' Seemingly nothing happens. Two men have an inconsequential conversation late at night in London.

They talk about:

- How busy the stall was – which is presumably important for the stall holder.
- When all the newspapers had been sold – ditto for the newspaper seller.
- 'George' and his arthritis (or not) – supposedly a common acquaintance.

Analysis

The most notable thing about the piece is the number of times the word 'Pause' appears.

What is the function the **theatrical technique** of the use of pauses?

It shows that the conversation is not flowing – that it appears to be about to die on its feet at any moment.

But the conversation does continue, because there is a 'hidden' conversation going on in parallel with the spoken words. This is often described as the **subtext**.

Dialogue, whether in Drama or in Fiction, can often say more in what is not being said than in what is actually being said. It is left to the audience (or the reader) to fill in the gaps.

In this sketch, who initiates the conversation?

In lines 1–5 the Man strikes up the conversation. The Barman's replies are not particularly enthusiastic – 'Ah.'; 'Ten, was it?' and the first little exchange grinds to a halt at the pause.

There has to be a thought passing through the mind of the Man before he says the next line.

It could be: *'I've tried that as a start-up line, I'll give him another go.'*

In lines 6–11 the Barman still does not appear terribly interested, but during the pause he presumably feels that because the Man has taken the trouble to talk about his business, he should at least respond.

Once you have realised the importance of the pauses, and that they have to be filled with a thought that enables the actor to move to the next line, you begin to see that there is something going on between the two which makes some sort of sense of the characterisation.

→

The **structure** of the sketch is rather like a short story.

The title is 'Last to go'.

Lines 1–51 provide the introduction to this idea.

Lines 52–78 are all about George.

Lines 79–97 tie up both *Last to Go* and George.

Up till now, you may have missed the **tone** of this piece. There is certainly something absurd going on:

- The idea that the 'Evening News' went 'Like a shot' seems incongruous.
- Lines 84–93 are also unconsciously absurd.
- And the final line reinforces to the audience the fact that 'George' was not in fact a common acquaintance.

There is obviously a lack of any real communication between the characters. The conversation is 'kept going' simply to fill time. It suggests that the central concern is that both men are quite isolated or bored, especially the Man – who seems to want the conversation to continue. Perhaps he is simply lonely and looking for any human contact, however unsatisfactory that might be.

Task

Actors must know what is going on in the pauses – what the subtext is. They must fill the pauses with thoughts which lead logically to their next utterance, otherwise their 'character' will not be convincing to the audience.

Try to fill all the pauses in *Last to Go* with the thoughts which might be running through the mind of the character who speaks next after each pause. This will give you insight into the characters.

For example:

- *Pause* (line 6)
  Man: (*thinking*) Is he listening to me, or what?
- *Pause* (line 11)
  Barman: (*thinking*) I suppose I'd better answer the old git – he might buy something.

Use of pause: creative writing

Having studied the use of the pause, the following little exercise might give you a start by looking at the different possibilities and different subtexts in a very small sequence.

Putting in pauses to create a subtext could create several different scenarios, for example:

Is that it?

Yes.

You're sure?

Yes.

Okay, let's go.

Is that it?

Pause

Yes.

Pause

You're sure?

Pause

Yes.

Pause

Okay, let's go.

Is that it?

Yes.

You're sure?

Pause

Yes.

Pause

Okay, let's go.

Task

With these ideas in mind, produce a short sketch, or the beginning of such a sketch.
The following is a student example of trying this technique.

The Decision

Oliver:	Is that it?	
	Pause	
Harry:	Yes.	
	Pause	
Oliver:	You're sure?	
	Pause	
Harry:	Yes.	
	Pause	
5	Oliver:	Okay, let's go.
	Pause	
	Are you sure this will work?	
Harry:	Of course it will.	
	Pause	
Oliver:	But we won't, like, get in trouble or anything?	
10	Harry:	No. As long as we stick to the plan and don't get caught.

Oliver: Caught? Who would catch us?

Pause

I thought you said she was out of town?   15

Pause

Harry: She is, I'm sure of it.

Oliver: But we can't like, get arrested, right?

Pause

Harry: Don't be stupid, it's harmless.   20

Oliver: She won't be, like mad?

Pause

Right?

Harry: Who cares if she's mad? She won't know it was us.   25

Oliver: Maybe she…

→

		Pause		I've got to do this.	
		I don't know about this.	Harry:	Okay. So you see that window?	
	Harry:	Oliver! We've come this far, don't even think about backing out now.		*Pause*	
30			Oliver:	Yeah.	45
		Pause	Harry:	That's hers.	
	Oliver:	You know what? You're right.		*Pause*	
		Pause	Oliver:	Are you sure?	
		It was a momentary lapse, that's all.		*Pause*	
35	Harry:	I hope so. This was your idea, Oli!	Oliver:	You know, we could like …	
				Pause	
	Oliver:	I know.		turn back?	
		Pause	Harry:	Stop being a baby and hand me the box.	50
		Maybe it was a bad idea, Harry.		*Pause*	
		Pause		Now pick one.	
40	Harry:	Just make a decision.		*Pause*	
		Pause		And do it.	
	Oliver:	I want to do this.	Oliver:	You do it!	
		Pause	Harry:	Oliver, just throw the damn egg!	55

Commentary

This little extract demonstrates the use of the pause reasonably well. The problem, of course, is that this sort of writing – a brief few lines, leading up to a mildly unexpected last line – is much more difficult to maintain over a longer sketch, with some sense of there being a central concern worth exploring.

For all drama writing check, by speaking the text out loud, that the dialogue sounds natural and credible.

Theatrical form: narrator/poetry/song

These theatrical techniques are used in the next extract from a play by Bertolt Brecht. He wanted to make political and social comment on society through the medium of drama. His use of a narrator (in this case The Singer and the Musicians) and his use of song and poetry, mixed with more prosaic dialogue, was designed to help the audience to stand back from the drama and see the plight of the protagonists intellectually rather than emotionally. There is much academic discussion of this idea, and some disagreement in the criticism of Brecht's plays, but the fact remains that the use of a narrator, or of heightened language, does cause a jolt – a sort of disconnect – within the audience which moves them away from the more conventional 'fourth wall' naturalistic drama. Thus it affects the audience's perception and reception of the play and its ideas.

There are parallels with certain aspects of fiction demonstrated in the section on narrative voice (pages 68–74).

The Caucasian Chalk Circle

In this play, written by Bertolt Brecht (1944–45) and translated by James and Tania Stern with
W.H. Auden, Grusha (the heroine, a servant girl) has reluctantly become responsible for the baby
son of the Governor, who was left carelessly by his selfish parents during a revolutionary uprising.
She has been travelling away from the city in order to find somewhere safe. She has just had to
escape from an inn where her identity has been questioned.

	Servant:	What's going on here?
	Elder Lady:	This person has smuggled herself in by playing the lady. She's probably a thief.
5	Young Lady:	And a dangerous one too. She wanted to murder us. It's a case for the police. Oh God, I can feel my migraine coming on!
	Servant:	There aren't any police at the moment. (*To Grusha*) Pack your things sister, and make yourself scarce.
	Grusha (*Angrily, picking up the child*):	You monsters! And they're already nailing your heads to the wall!
10	Servant (*pushing her out*):	Shut your trap. Or you'll have the Old Man here. And there's no trifling with him.
	Elder Lady (*to the younger lady*):	Just see if she hasn't stolen something already!
		(*While the ladies are looking, the servant and Grusha leave*)
	Servant:	Look before you leap, I say. Another time have a good look at people before you get mixed up with them.
15	Grusha:	I thought they'd be more likely to treat their own kind better.
	Servant:	Not them! Believe me, nothing's harder than aping a lazy useless person. Once they suspect you can wipe your own arse, or that your hands ever touched a broom, the game's up. Just wait a minute, I'll get you a corn cake and a few apples.
20	Grusha:	Better not. I must get out before the Old Man comes. And if I walk all night I'll be out of danger, I think.
		(*She walks away*)
	Servant (*calling after her in a low voice*):	At the next crossroads, turn right.
		(*Grusha disappears*)
	The Singer:	As Grusha Vachnadze wandered northwards
		She was followed by the Prince's Ironshirts.
25	Musicians:	How will the barefooted girl escape the Ironshirts
		The bloodhounds, the trappers?
		They are hunting even by night.
		Pursuers don't get tired.
		Butchers sleep little
		(*The Ironshirts are trudging along the highway*)

→

30	Corporal:	Blockhead, you'll never amount to anything. Why? Because your heart's not in it. Your superior sees it in little things. Yesterday when I laid that fat woman, I admit you collared her husband as I commanded. And you did kick him in the stomach. But did you enjoy it like a good soldier? Or did you just do it from a sense of duty? I've kept my eyes on you, blockhead. You're like a hollow reed or a tinkling cymbal. You'll never get promoted. *(They walk a while in silence)* Don't you get the idea I don't notice how insubordinate you are in every way. I forbid you to limp! You do it simply because I sold the horses, and I sold them because I'd never have got that price again. I know you: you limp just to show me you don't like marching. But that won't help you. It'll go against you. Sing!
	2 Ironshirts *(singing)*:	O sadly one morning, one morning in May
		I kissed my darling and rode far away.
		Protect her dear friends, until home from the wars
45		I come riding in triumph, alive on my horse.
	Corporal:	Louder!
	2 Ironshirts:	When I lie in my grave and my sword turns to rust
		My darling shall bring me a handful of dust
		For the feet that so gaily ran up to her door
50		And the arms that went round her shall please her no more.
		(They walk on in silence)
	Corporal:	A good soldier has his heart and soul in it. He lets himself be hacked to pieces by his superiors, and even while dying he's aware of his Corporal nodding approval. For him that's reward enough. That's all he wants. But you won't get a nod. And you'll croak just the same. Christ, how am I to lay my hands on the Governor's bastard with an ass like you!
		(They trudge on)
	The Singer:	When Grusha Vachnadze came to the River Sirra
		The flight grew too much for her, the helpless child too heavy.
	Musicians:	The rosy dawn in the cornfields
60		Is nothing but cold to the sleepless.
		The gay clatter of the milk cans in the farmyard
		Where the smoke rises is nothing but a threat to the fugitives.
		She who drags the child feels nothing but its weight.
		(Grusha stops in front of a farm)
	Grusha:	Now you've wetted yourself again, and you know I've no nappies. Michael, we've got to part. This is far enough from the city. They won't want you so badly, little squirt, that they'll follow you all this way. The woman looks kind, and just you smell the milk! So farewell, little Michael. I'll forget how you kicked me in the back all

70   night to make me go faster. And you – you forget the meagre fare. It was meant well. I'd love to have kept you, because your nose is so small, but it can't be done. I'd have shown you your first rabbit and – how not to wet yourself, but I must turn back, because my sweetheart the soldier might soon return, and suppose he didn't find me? You can't ask that of me, Michael.

(A fat peasant woman carries a milk can to the door. Grusha waits till she has gone in, and lays the child on the threshold. Then, hiding, she waits until the woman opens the door and sees the bundle.)

75   **Woman:**   Jesus Christ, what's this? Husband!

Husband: What's up? Let me have my soup.

Woman
(to the child):   Where's your mother? Haven't you got one? It's a boy. And the linen is fine; it's from a good family. And they just leave him on our doorstep. Oh, what times we live in!

80   **Husband:**   If they think we're going to feed it, they're mistaken. You take it to the priest in the village. That's all we can do.

Woman: What will the priest do with it? It needs a mother. There, it's waking up. Don't you think we could keep it?

Husband: No!

85   **Woman:**   I could lay it in the corner, next to the armchair. I only need a crib for it. Look how it's smiling! Husband, we have a roof over our heads and we can do it. I won't hear another word.

(She carries the child into the house. Grusha steps out, laughs and hurries away.)

The Singer: Why so gay, you, making for home?

Musicians: Because with a smile the child

90   Has won new parents for himself, that's why I'm gay.

Because I am rid of the loved one

That's why I am happy.

The Singer: And why are you sad?

Musicians: I'm sad because I'm single and free

95   Of the little burden in whom a heart was beating:

Like one robbed, like one impoverished I'm going.

Task

Think about how the use of narrative devices of poetry and song in this scene affect the audience's understanding of the situation Grusha is in. Mark up your text accordingly.

Initial thoughts

The Singer and Musicians provide the factual narrative for the plot – and enable the stage to be transformed into wherever they say it is.

Grusha leaves an inn and travels (many miles?) through cornfields, crosses a river and reaches a farmhouse where she leaves Michael. There can be no attempt to show this on stage, unless film/back projection is used – which is an equally 'non-naturalistic' method of narration.

It allows the writer to 'short-circuit' all the details of the journey and the necessity to 'show' the scenery.

Analysis

The narrative voices, The Singer and the Musicians do more than provide the audience with the details of the journey, such as:

The Singer: When Grusha Vachnadze came to the River Sirra

The flight grew too much for her, the helpless child too heavy. (57–58)

They also let us into Grusha's thoughts and emotions:

Musicians: I'm sad because I'm single and free

Of the little burden in whom a heart was beating:

Like one robbed, like one impoverished I'm going. (94–96)

The reference in line 26 to 'The bloodhounds, the trappers' introduces the Ironshirts in all their military 'glory'. The Corporal's speech very quickly deals with rape and corruption in the pursuit of 'duty' and insists that the other two soldiers 'Sing'.

But the song, although it starts by sounding relatively happy in the first verse, ends with their graves in the second verse. In this way, Brecht uses the force of traditional folk song/tale to encapsulate the ever-present, universal soldier's tale – triumph and hopeful heroism followed by death and isolation.

The use of poetry allows for an emphasis on the burden that Grusha has been carrying:

Musicians: The rosy dawn in the cornfields

Is nothing but cold to the sleepless.

The gay clatter of the milk cans in the farmyard

Where the smoke rises is nothing but a threat to the fugitives.

She who drags the child feels nothing but its weight. (59–63)

where the repetition in 'nothing but cold', 'nothing but a threat', 'nothing but its weight' is seen as pulling her body and spirit down to the ground.

And again in:

Musicians: …

That's why I am happy.

The Singer: And why are you sad? (92–93)

where her dilemma is encapsulated in two lines.

In a way we, the audience, are aligned with the narrators, and are looking at Grusha's behaviour as told to us, rather than living her experience with her, as in a more conventional narrative. Brecht's idea was that this method would allow an audience to take a more impartial view of the action on stage.

Thus, we should notice the appalling behaviour of the Corporal, and the way in which his men are forced to collude with him.

We should be looking at the effects of the class divide illustrated in the opening of this extract, and the common cause made by 'the workers' (the servant and Grusha) against them.

And we should notice the humanity displayed by the peasant woman to the abandoned child:

'Husband, we have a roof over our heads and we can do it.'

Summary

The use of a narrator – or in this case two narrative 'voices' – makes a difference to the audience's understanding of the plot and to the audience's emotional connection with the characters.

The use of song and poetry has an effect on the way in which the audience appreciates the concerns of the play.

Note: The role of the narrator is effective when it has a purpose which is greater than merely providing a lazy shortcut for the dramatist.

Use of narrator/poetry/song: creative writing

Having studied these scenes, with the focus on characterisation, the next task is for you to attempt writing a script for yourself.

Then, you should apply the same skills of analysis to your own (or your fellow students') work by editing.

The High Snow

	Narr:	A little scenario: a snowy scene, a steep mountain path, a heavily burdened Sherpa – and – a little behind – our man, bearded, wearing tweeds and stout nailed boots, upright, tall and free.
5	Man:	How much further? According to my map you should be reaching a plateau.
	Sherpa:	That is possible. The map in my head is older than yours or you, or me. It comes to me from my ancestors.
	Man:	Stop talking rubbish. This is not a game.
		Pause
10	Sherpa:	In the game that is life, you have barely finished your first hand –
	Narr:	The man stops. The Sherpa does not. The mountain towers higher, the light closes closer – and the burden remains just as heavy.
	Man:	Stop. We are off my route.
15	Sherpa:	(*stopping*) But not mine, or the guardians of our motherland. We may bear the white man's burden, but we do not follow his ways.
	Man:	I order you to follow my map. This is not a game.
20	Sherpa:	– and you are nowhere in the race that is the game.
	Narr:	The Sherpa moves off higher into the mist, the home of his gods. The man must, perforce, follow. He carries no burden. But he cannot survive without one.
25	Sherpa:	As for those who think they can leave the table with a game in progress which sucks them in –
	Man:	Will you …
30	Sherpa:	will find the odds may turn against them in the course of the game.
		Pause
	Man:	I order you to stop this game.
35	Narr:	This is an impasse. The Sherpa stops. The darkness falls. They both wait.
	Man:	I will take some of the burden.
	Sherpa:	Too little, too late. Your map is not mine

➜

your way is not mine

40   your gods are not mine.

Narr: The Sherpa moves on. Our man struggles on after him, bent as under a burden, into the dark. ~~Looks like he is going to have to rely on the game of life dealing him a good hand.~~ The hand he has been dealt by the gods may – or may not – be a good one.

Commentary

In this little sketch, the Narrator's words (in blue) have a function to fulfil, apart from the setting of the scene. He is making a political comment about colonialism – exploitation of other races, etc.

The metaphor of the 'game' (of cards presumably) is sustained, but the Narrator's last phrase (in green) is not in the correct register – it is too modern for the supposed scenario, which must be somewhere in the nineteenth or early twentieth century (according to the mountaineering dress of the Man). It has been replaced by a new, more suitable, sentence.

The 'poetry' (in green) of the Sherpa's dialogue about the 'game of life' has, in fact, no real 'poetic' quality. Nothing is gained by putting these comments in lines – except, perhaps, for his last speech.

For all drama writing check, by speaking the text out loud, that the dialogue sounds natural and credible.

PART TWO

PRACTICE PIECES

Introduction

There are some pieces of general advice which apply to all the genres in this section.

1   Read the context at the top of the passage – there will be information on title, writer, genre (important for fiction and non-fiction) and date of publication.
2   Turn to the end of the passage, and read the question carefully.

These two very simple steps will give you some idea of what to look for even in your first reading.

3   Mark up the passage/poem in the way that you are used to.
4   Have a tick list in your head of the techniques you might be required to cover. This will vary from genre to genre, but will include such important aspects as characterisation, persona, structure, language and so on.
5   Make sure you have considered the TONE of the passage/poem – have you missed something important, such as humour, or self-reflection or despair?
6   In generating your response, remember to provide supporting evidence for your statements/ opinions/guesses/evaluation.
7   Don't spend so much time on the beginning that you fail to give the end of the passage/poem proper consideration. Often the real point of the passage is contained in its conclusion.

> A range of points for each practice piece, at least some of which you should have covered, can be found on the Hodder Gibson website at www.hoddereducation.co.uk/ updatesandextras. For each piece there is also an evaluative student response and commentary.

Note: These passages and the associated student responses on the website are shorter than is usual in the final exam paper, but they should allow you to practise the analytical skills you have learned.

Poetry

Read *Mercies* by Don Paterson (2015) and then answer the question which follows it.

Mercies

She might have had months left of her dog-years,
but to be who? She'd grown light as a nest
and spent the whole day under her long ears
listening to the bad radio in her breast.

5   On the steel bench, knowing what was taking shape
she tried and tried to stand, as if to sign
that she was still of use, and should escape
our selection. So I turned her face to mine,
and seeing only love there – which, for all

10   the wolf in her, she knew as well as we did –
she lay back down and let the needle enter.
And love was surely what her eyes concede
as her stare grew hard, and one bright aerial
quit making its report back to the centre.

Question

Write a critical evaluation of *Mercies* in which you show how effectively the poetic techniques have helped you to appreciate the central concern.

Poetry

Read the following poem by Fleur Adcock (1974) and then answer the question which follows it.

Kilpeck

We are dried and brittle this morning,

fragile with continence, quiet.

You have brought me to see a church.

I stare at a Norman arch in red sandstone

5   carved like a Mayan temple-gate;

at serpents writhing up the doorposts

and squat saints with South-American features

who stare back over our heads

from a panel of beasts and fishes.

10   The gargoyles jutting from under the eaves

are the colour of newborn children.

Last night you asked me

if poetry was the most important thing.

We walk on around the building

15   craning our heads back to look up

at lions, griffins, fat-faced bears.

The Victorians broke some of these figures

as being too obscene for a church;

but they missed the Whore of Kilpeck.

20   She leans out under the roof

holding her pink stony cleft agape

with her ancient little hands.

There was always witchcraft here, you say.

The sheep-track up to the fragments

25   of castle-wall is fringed with bright bushes.

We clamber awkwardly, separate.

Hawthorn and dog rose offer hips and haws,

orange and crimson capsules pretending

harvest. I taste a blackberry.

30   The soil here is coloured like brick-dust,

like the warm sandstone. A fruitful county.

We regard it uneasily.

→

There is little left to say

after all the talk we had last night

35   instead of going to bed –

fearful for our originality,

avoiding the sweet obvious act

as if it were the only kind of indulgence.

Silly, perhaps.

40   We have our reward.

We are languorous now, heavy

with whatever we were conserving,

carrying each a delicate burden

of choices made or about to be made.

45   Words whisper hopefully in our heads.

Slithering down the track we hold hands

to keep a necessary balance.

The gargoyles extend their feral faces,

rosy, less lined than ours.

50   We are wearing our identities.

Question

Show how effectively Fleur Adcock employs poetic techniques to enhance your appreciation of the ideas she expresses in *Kilpeck*.

Prose fiction

Read the following extract from *The Pyramid* by William Golding (1967) and then answer the question which follows it.

The Pyramid

It was really summer, but the rain had fallen all day and was still falling. The weather can best be described by saying it was the kind best reserved for church fêtes. The green leaves were being beaten off the trees by the steady downpour and were drifting about in the puddles. Now and then there would come a gust of wind so that the trees moaned

5   and tossed their arms imploringly, though they had been rooted in our soil long enough to know better. Darkness fell early – indeed there had seemed little light all day, so the process was slow and imperceptible. But when it was complete, the darkness was intense beyond the street lights and the rain still fell through it. I had played the piano until my head sang – pounded savagely and unavailingly at the C Minor Study of Chopin which

10   had seemed, when Moisewitch played, to express all the width and power of my own love, my own hopeless infatuation. But Imogen was engaged to be married, that was the end.

So I lay, dry-mouthed and endured. The only thing that pulled me out of myself every now and then was the sudden sound of blown water, dashed over the panes like gravel. Eighteen is a good time for suffering. One has all the necessary strength, and no

15   defences. Midnight clanged from the tower of the church, and before the twelfth stroke had sounded, the three sodium lights in the Square went out. In my head, Imogen drove in his green, open Lagonda across the downs, her long, reddish hair flying back from her pale face – she was only five years older than I was. I ought to have done something; and now it was too late. I stared at the invisible ceiling, and she drove; and I saw him,

20   so secure, so old, so huge in his ownership of The Stillbourne Advertiser, impregnable. I heard his gnatlike voice and suddenly he was struck by lightning. I saw it branch down, there was a puff of smoke and he was gone. Somehow, the lightning had rendered Imogen insensible. I was carrying her in my arms.

I leapt up in bed, staring at the window, and clutching the counterpane to my chin.

25   The noise had been so loud, so sharp. It rapped the glass almost to breaking point, as if someone had used an air-gun. I had hazy thoughts of blown branches or dislodged tiles but knew it had been neither – and there it was again, rap! I huddled out of bed, my hair pricking at the strangeness, went to the window and peered down into the Square. There was another rap close by my face, so that I ducked, then peered forward; and just

30   outside the railings that separated our cottage from the cobbles round the Square I could see a white face glimmering. I eased up the sash and immediately the wind whipped the chintz curtains in my face.

'Oliver! Oliver!'

A wild hope made my heart turn over; but it was not Imogen's voice.

35   It was Evie Babbacombe.

Question

How effective is this passage in giving the reader insights into Oliver's character? Consider not only characterisation, but also setting, tone and narrative voice.

Prose non-fiction

The following extract was written in 2015 by Adrian Gill, restaurant reviewer and TV critic for *The Sunday Times*. Read the extract and then answer the question which follows.

Why I Can't Write

St Christopher School in Letchworth, Hertfordshire, was a Quaker school that prided itself on finding the inner man or woman in the most unpromising children. It was also one of the only institutions in the country that claimed to be able to cure dyslexia. It was fee-paying and private.

5   We couldn't really afford school fees and those at St Christopher were particularly excessive, but again there was the absolute belief in the absolute goodness of education. My parents agreed to find them. My mother was sent back to work. (She was an actress, my father made documentaries.)

Neither of them ever mentioned the money, never made me feel responsible or guilty or
10 indebted, but of course I knew. Not least because boarding school was never an option for my brother Nick.

My mother took me to school. A matron showed the bunk beds that I would share with three other boys in a cold and grubby threadbare hut. I went back outside to say goodbye to my mother but she had already left. I expect she didn't want to upset me by seeing
15 her cry. I sat on my bed and have never felt quite so utterly, desperately alone. I swore an oath that I would never, ever send a child of mine away.

I also decided that I should be someone else – to pretend to be someone I wasn't, because who I was was bullied and friendless and plainly failing.

And somehow it worked. Like a spy in deep cover, I am still pretending to be the person
20 I made up on a dreary Sunday in September. This character liked being around girls and discovered that he was popular. Within a term his stammer had been swallowed whole.

St Christopher was both utterly bizarre and spot on the 1960s zeitgeist. Unusually for boarding schools then, but as a great consolation to us, it was co-educational. It was also vegetarian. And organic.

25 We could wear what we liked, though strangely not jeans. We could grow our hair as long as we wished … which was long. The school prided itself on listening to children and that everyone's voice carried equal weight, so we were self-governing.

No one ever mentioned dyslexia. St Christopher had no real – or even unreal – idea of how to teach those with learning difficulties. There was no cure and no dedicated staff,
30 no plan, no joined-up thought. Just a general woolly belief in finding your inner spelling bee, helped by the nice plump woman.

The school may have sold my parents a wishful lie, but essentially all schools that claimed to help alleviate or extinguish word blindness or innumeracy are still offering patent lies.

35 In the end it always comes down to the nice plump woman who sits with you, and in a kindly, prodding voice, suggests you try again … but concentrate this time. The plump lady is not there for the child's support, she is there for the schools to show that they're on it. Getting it fixed.

➔

40 Still the medicine given to dyslexic children is more work, extra writing, remedial reading, more numbers ... the utter abysmal useless cruelty of this has never occurred to a teacher. To compound failure with repeated failure reaffirms this humiliation and the fear and the loathing for words and learning, constantly pushing a door marked 'Lupl'.

Ironically, a dyslexic does learn. We learn a series of sleights and misdirections to get us through the misery of the special slow 'try again' learning. I watched my son doing it. He

45 relies on your impatience because, with the best will in the world, teachers, particularly kindly plump women, will encourage by offering hints, noises and vowel sounds. They can't stand the suspense of the fact that we can fail to recognise a word that we managed a moment ago.

The child learns to decipher these with a lightning speed, then gets the word right or

50 will rattle a stream of possibilities till they hear the squeak of congratulation that gives the teacher a little glow of pleasure, because she's taught well. The recognised word is her little success and the dyslexic will continue to encourage the plump woman, will help and reward her with the right word and a big smile that looks like gratitude but is actually pity because we have found someone who's worse at what they do than we are.

55 Essentially a dyslexic child will cajole adults into reading for him and will also listen to other children to learn content. My eldest son can have knowledgeable conversations about the entire Harry Potter series without having read one and both my boys have learnt to radiate an ungainsayable, granite-melting charm that slides them through classes on casters made of flattery.

60 I spent my time in the art room because that's where dyslexics go to paint, or the pottery shed, the carpentry workshop, the dance studio, the music room. These are the corners of the academic world that don't deal in letters and numbers.

My real passion was history. I loved it. It was the only subject I worked hard at. Our history teacher, 'Gammy' Mercer, a malevolent, bitterly mean man with a withered

65 hand, consistently marked my homework as failed. After a couple of years I was upset and disheartened enough to stay behind and ask him – not an easy thing; he didn't like pupils and was terse and sarcastic – 'Why do you mark me so badly? I know my history is better than this.'

'Your history? Oh, your history. Yes, you're one of the best in the class at history. I'm

70 marking you the way an examiner will. You have a problem with your writing.' And he walked off.

I thought: 'Actually, you know, I don't have a problem with my writing ... you've got a problem with my writing. Fuck you. I'm never going to let this be my problem ever again.'

And I never have. I've always made it someone else's.

Questions

Discuss the effectiveness of the ways in which Gill reflects upon this personal experience. You should think particularly about the persona that he establishes in the essay and the tone which he adopts.

Drama

The following extract is from *A Doll's House* by Henrik Ibsen (1879). Read the extract and then answer the question which follows it.

Nora has just been visited by Krogstad, who threatens to blackmail her over the fact that she had (innocently) forged her father's signature on a document. If she doesn't persuade her husband – the new acting bank manager – not to sack him, Krogstad will reveal everything.

A Doll's House

	Nora:	*(begins dressing the tree)* A candle here—and flowers here—The horrible man! It's all nonsense — there's nothing wrong. The tree shall be splendid! I will do everything I can think of to please you, Torvald! — I will sing for you, dance for you — *(TORVALD comes in with some papers under his arm.)* Oh! Are you
5		back already?
	Torv:	Yes. Has anyone been here?
	Nora:	Here? No.
	Torv:	That is strange. I saw Krogstad going out of the gate.
	Nora:	Did you? Oh yes, I forgot, Krogstad was here for a moment.
10	Torv:	Nora, I can see from your manner that he has been here begging you to say a good word for him.
	Nora:	Yes.
	Torv:	And you were to appear to do it of your own accord; you were to conceal from me the fact of his having been here; didn't he beg that of you too?
15	Nora:	Yes, Torvald, but—
	Torv:	Nora, Nora, and you would be a party to that sort of thing? To have any talk with a man like that, and give him any sort of promise? And to tell me a lie into the bargain?
	Nora:	A lie—?
20	Torv:	Didn't you tell me no one had been here? *(Shakes his finger at her.)* My little songbird must never do that again. A songbird must have a clean beak to chirp with—no false notes! *(Puts his arm round her waist.)* That is so, isn't it? Yes, I am sure it is. *(Lets her go.)* We will say no more about it. How warm and snug it is here!
25	Nora	*(after a short pause, during which she busies herself with the Christmas Tree)* Torvald!
	Torv:	Yes
	Nora:	I am looking forward tremendously to the fancy-dress ball at the Stenborgs' the day after tomorrow.
30	Torv:	And I am tremendously curious to see what you are going to surprise me with.
	Nora:	It was very silly of me to want to do that.
	Torv:	What do you mean?

→

	Nora:	I can't hit upon anything that will do; everything I think of seems so silly and insignificant.
35	Torv:	Does my little Nora acknowledge that at last?
	Nora:	Are you very busy, Torvald?
	Torv:	Well—
	Nora:	What are all those papers?
	Torv:	Bank business.
40	Nora:	Already?
	Torv:	I have got authority from the retiring manager to undertake the necessary changes in the staff and in the rearrangement of the work; and I must make use of the Christmas week for that, so as to have everything in order for the new year.
45	Nora:	Then that was why this poor Krogstad—
	Torv:	Hm!
	Nora:	*(leans against the back of his chair and strokes his hair)* If you hadn't been so busy I should have asked you a tremendously big favour, Torvald.
	Torv:	What is that? Tell me.
50	Nora:	There is no one has such good taste as you. And I do so want to look nice at the fancy-dress ball. Torvald, couldn't you take me in hand and decide what I shall go as, and what sort of a dress I shall wear?
	Torv:	Aha! so my obstinate little woman is obliged to get someone to come to her rescue?
55	Nora:	Yes, Torvald, I can't get along a bit without your help.
	Torv:	Very well, I will think it over, we shall manage to hit upon something.
	Nora:	That is nice of you. *(Goes to the Christmas Tree. A short pause.)* How pretty the red flowers look. But tell me, was it really something very bad that this Krogstad was guilty of?
60	Torv:	He forged someone's name. Have you any idea what that means?
	Nora:	Isn't it possible that he was driven to do it by necessity?
	Torv:	Yes; or, as in so many cases, by imprudence. I am not so heartless as to condemn a man altogether because of a single false step of that kind.
	Nora:	No, you wouldn't, would you, Torvald?
65	Torv:	Many a man has been able to retrieve his character, if he has openly confessed his fault and taken his punishment.
	Nora:	Punishment—?
	Torv:	But Krogstad did nothing of that sort; he got himself out of it by a cunning trick, and that is why he has gone under altogether.
70	Nora:	But do you think it would—?
	Torv:	Just think how a guilty man like that has to lie and play the hypocrite with every one, how he has to wear a mask in the presence of those near and dear to him, even before his own wife and children. And about the children—that is the most terrible part of it all, Nora.

75	Nora:	How?
	Torv:	Because such an atmosphere of lies infects and poisons the whole life of a home. Each breath the children take in such a house is full of the germs of evil.
	Nora:	*(coming nearer him)* Are you sure of that?
80	Torv:	My dear, I have often seen it in the course of my life as a lawyer. Almost everyone who has gone to the bad early in life has had a deceitful mother.
	Nora:	Why do you only say—mother?
85	Torv:	It seems most commonly to be the mother's influence, though naturally a bad father's would have the same result. Every lawyer is familiar with the fact. This Krogstad, now, has been persistently poisoning his own children with lies and dissimulation; that is why I say he has lost all moral character. *(Holds out his hands to her.)* That is why my sweet little Nora must promise me not to plead his cause. Give me your hand on it. Come, come, what is this? Give me your hand. There now, that's settled. I assure you it would be quite impossible for me to work with him; I literally feel physically ill when I am in the company of such people.
90		
	Nora:	*(takes her hand out of his and goes to the opposite side of the Christmas Tree)* How hot it is in here; and I have such a lot to do.
95	Torv:	*(getting up and putting his papers in order)* Yes, and I must try and read through some of these before dinner; and I must think about your costume, too. And it is just possible I may have something ready in gold paper to hang up on the Tree. *(Puts his hand on her head.)* My precious little singing-bird! *(He goes out shutting the door.)*
	Nora:	*(after a pause, whispers)* No, no—it isn't true. It's impossible; it must be impossible.
100		*(The Nurse opens the door on the left.)*
	Nurse:	The little ones are begging so hard to be allowed to come in to mamma.
	Nora:	No, no, no! Don't let them come in to me! You stay with them, Anne.
	Nurse:	Very well, ma'am. *(Shuts the door.)*
105	Nora:	*(pale with terror)* Deprave my little children? Poison my home? *(A short pause. Then she tosses her head.)* It's not true. It can't possibly be true.

Question

Write a detailed analysis of the means by which Ibsen presents the relationship between Nora and Torvald in this scene. You should consider not only characterisation, but also dramatic structure.

Acknowledgements

p.1 Extract from The Guardian. Copyright © 2008 by Zadie Smith. Reproduced by permission of the author c/o Rogers, Coleridge & White Ltd., 20 Powis Mews, London W11 1JN;

p.2 Billy Collins, excerpt from 'Introduction to Poetry' from *The Apple That Astonished Paris*. Copyright © 1988, 1996 by Billy Collins. Reprinted with the permission of The Permissions Company, Inc., on behalf of the University of Arkansas Press, www.uapress.com;

p.3 William Shakespeare (out of copyright);

pp.8 and 9 'Design', in *Selected Poems of Robert Frost*, p.198. Used by permission.;

p.9 Robert Frost (1922), 'In White' in *Modern American Poets* (ed. Robert Diyanni), p.89;

pp.11 and 36–37 Lawrence Ferlinghetti, from *A Coney Island of the Mind: Poems*. Copyright © 1958 by Lawrence Ferlinghetti. Reprinted by permission of New Directions Publishing Corp.;

pp.14 and 37 'Child on Top of a Greenhouse', in *Words for the Wind: The Collected Verse of Theodore Roethke*. Copyright © 1961 by Theodore Roethke.;

pp.17–18 'Diving into the Wreck'. Copyright © 2016 by the Adrienne Rich Literary Trust. Copyright © 1973 by W.W. Norton & Company, Inc., from Collected Poems: 1950–2012 by Adrienne Rich. Used by permission of W.W. Norton & Company, Inc.;

p.23 'To My Favourite 17-Year Old High School Girl', in *Aimless Love* by Billy Collins. Copyright © 2013 by Billy Collins.;

pp.24–25 *To Autumn* by John Keats (out of copyright);

p.29 and 38 *Meeting at Night* by Robert Browning (out of copyright);

p.30 'One Art' from *POEMS* by Elizabeth Bishop. Copyright © 2011 by The Alice H. Methfessel Trust. Publisher's Note and compilation copyright © 2011 by Farrar, Straus and Giroux, LLC. Reprinted by permission of Farrar, Straus and Giroux, LLC.;

pp.39–40 and 42–43 *The Grown-ups* by Victoria Glendinning. Copyright © 1989 by Victoria Glendinning. Reproduced by permission of Simon & Schuster and David Higham Associates Ltd.;

pp.45–46 *The Actor* by Stan Barstow. Copyright © by Stan Barstow.;

pp.49–50 *Dombey and Son* by Charles Dickens (out of copyright);

pp.55–57 *The Breadwinner* by Leslie Halward. Copyright © 1936 Leslie Halward. Reprinted by permission of David Higham Associates Ltd.;

pp.59–60 *Maurice* by E.M. Forster. Copyright © 1971 The Provost and Scholars of King's College, Cambridge. Reproduced by permission of Hodder and Stoughton Limited.;

p.63 *Ancestors* by Virginia Woolf (reproduced under fair dealing);

p.64 Excerpt from *The Handmaid's Tale* by Margaret Atwood. Copyright © 1986 O.W. Toad, Ltd. Reprinted by permission of Houghton Mifflin Harcourt Publishing Company. All rights reserved.;

p.68 *One Flew Over The Cuckoo's Nest* by Ken Kesey. Copyright © 1962 by Ken Kesey.;

p.70 *The Remains of the Day* by Kazuo Ishiguro. Copyright © 1989 by Kazuo Ishiguro.;

p.71 *Enduring Love* by Ian McEwan. Copyright © 1997 by Ian McEwan.;

pp.72–73 *A Tradition of Eighteen Hundred and Four* by Thomas Hardy (out of copyright);

p.73 *Vanity Fair* by W.M. Thackery (out of copyright);

p.74 *Molloy* by Samuel Beckett. Copyright © 1951 by Samuel Beckett.;